DR DALE is the founder of the School of Survival, a society of experts who live for one purpose only: to train the masses to survive the rising of the undead and other (currently) fictitious and mythological creatures. Based on his sell-out Edinburgh festival show and nationwide tour, *Dr Dale's Zombie Dictionary* is a must-read if you plan on surviving a zombie apocalypse.

www.howtosurviveazombieapocalypse.co.uk

Dr Dale's

ZOMBIE DICTIONARY

The A-Z Guide to Staying Alive

DR DALE SESLICK

Illustrated by Jack Knight

This edition first published in 2010 by
Allison & Busby Limited
13 Charlotte Mews
London, W1T 4EJ
www.allisonandbusby.com

A CIP catalogue record for this book is available from
the British Library.

10 9 8 7 6 5 4 3

ISBN 978-0-7490-0805-5

Typeset in 11/14.5 pt Garamond by
Allison & Busby Ltd.

The paper used for this Allison & Busby publication
has been produced from trees that have been legally sourced
from well-managed and credibly certified forests.

Printed and bound by CPI Group (UK) Ltd, Croydon, CR0 4YY

Disclaimer: While clearly a work of humour, this book
is also a work of fiction, and its author and publisher
assume no liability for readers who act upon the fictive
instructions herein.

Dedication

Dr Dale wishes to thank all those who have been integral to the research that is included in this edition.

With special consideration to Donald, Judy and Tristen for their continuing hard work and dedication.

And the random homeless people who gave their time and bodies for a plate of sandwiches in order for us to carry out experiments on them, in the current absence of any undead.

Keep vigilant and stay safe.

INTRODUCTION

Hi, I'm Dr Dale from Dr Dale's School of Survival, and I've written this book to make sure you don't get your intestines ripped out.

First of all, let me thank you for buying my *Zombie Dictionary*, for taking this positive step to guarantee your own survival should the undead rise. You should take a moment now to feel a great sense of inner peace, satisfied that you had the foresight and strength to admit that you needed the *Zombie Dictionary* in order to prepare for the zombie apocalypse. You needed Dr Dale's help. Yes, that's it, let that cosy feeling of needing me just flow right through you.

OK, that's enough inner peace and self satisfaction. We should really get down to the business of making sure you don't die... And rise again.

Those of you who have purchased this book in the hope of finding out all about the best firearms, heavy artillery, torpedoes, missiles, tanks and submarines will be sorely disappointed. Here at the School of Survival, those are not the kind of methods we use. During a zombie apocalypse, guns will be in short supply – they also require ammunition and constant maintenance to make sure they are at peak performance. All this means that they are unreliable. You need to learn how to survive using anything and everything you can get your hands on as well as a healthy dose of common sense, and that is what we shall be focusing on in these pages.

Throughout this dictionary there will be facts that will shock, astound and amaze you in equal measure – but be aware that none of the advice can be taken as definitive. As yet, no zombies have risen from the grave on which to test our theories. However, like most resourceful, intelligent people, here at the school we have researched our information thoroughly using movies, books, blogs, forums, Wikipedia and a man down the pub who we think is called Bob...or perhaps Bert – can't really remember, but he does wear a hat.

We hope you have an informative and life-changing journey with us through the pages of the *Zombie Dictionary* and if, in fact, this information turns out not to be useful and you don't survive a zombie apocalypse, we are happy to give you a full no-qualms refund if the book is returned within 30 days of purchase, with a valid receipt, by the person who bought it.

ZOMBIES:
THE BASICS

As many of you know, the word zombies begins with a Z which is the last letter of the alphabet and though some of you may find it too radical a step to cope with at this stage of your training I am going to cover 'the Z word' first as I feel it's important we all know what we're dealing with.

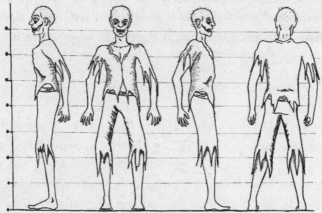

There is certain knowledge that I will take for granted during the book as I assume you are all aware of the basics of Zombie Mythology. For those who aren't, here's a brief introduction:

1) A Zombie is dead!

In recent films and in the media (*28 Days Later* and *Left 4 Dead*) zombies have been portrayed as humans who have become infected with some form of virus that has made them crave human flesh and become a bit grumpy. These are not zombies. These are people who want to eat other live human beings and are more commonly referred to as cannibals (and this is not the *Dictionary of Cannibal Survival* – that book will be available soon). The only zombies being dealt with in these pages are those that have been previously human, became infected, died and reanimated again.

2) A Zombie bite is infectious.

There are various ways in which a human can become a zombie (see **Classification**) but we do know one thing for sure. If you are bitten by a zombie you will die and rise again as a zombie yourself. Zombies attack with their mouths and this has given rise to the misconception that they are trying to 'eat' you. As the zombies' digestive system is no longer operational it is highly unlikely that this is the case. The instinct to bite is merely the virus's way of spreading and increasing the zombie masses.

3) Zombies can only be 'killed' by destroying the brain.

A zombie's Achilles heel is not its heel but its brain and the only way to destroy a zombie is to destroy its brain. As all other bodily functions and systems shut down on death, the only thing that keeps the zombie going is its brain. This means that zombies are impervious to pain so will keep coming until you achieve a head shot (the reason you go for a head shot is that the brain is kept in the head – that's the round thing on your neck with hair on top and a face on the front). This is why your choice of weapon is important – but more of that later.

4) There is no cure.

There is no cure for a zombie infection. Once you are bitten, you become a zombie. So stop thinking there is a cure because there isn't. Even if there is it's important that you think there isn't. Because thinking there's a cure will give you hope, and hope will make you weak, and weakness will make you lose, and losing mean you die, and dying means you rise, and rising means you become a zombie – for which there is no cure. So stop thinking there's a cure because that will give you hope and hope will make you weak and... You get the message.

Those are the basics of zombies and that is all you need to know so far. Don't worry about *why* the dead have started to rise or indeed *how* the dead have started to rise. Once they rise it does become somewhat of a moot point. Your only concern once the apocalypse begins is to *survive* – not to question the whole affair.

Remember, the zombies won't be bothered why it happened – they'll just be focused on biting you. You need to focus too. On living.

Let us continue...

AARDVARK

In African folklore the aardvark is much admired because of its diligent quest for food and its fearless response to the strong, warlike soldier ant. In the event of a zombie apocalypse, we should all take a lesson from the humble aardvark in order to survive, using the analogy that you are an aardvark and the undead hordes are a swarm of warrior ants. Do not take this analogy too far though, as zombies cannot be killed with Nippon.

African Hausa magicians make charms from the heart, skin, forehead and nails of the aardvark, which are then pounded together with the root of a certain tree. Wrapped in a piece of skin and worn on the chest, the charm is said to give the owner the ability to pass through walls or roofs at night.

Should you happen to come across an aardvark during the apocalypse and wish to try this technique, we recommend getting a friend you are not terribly fond of to attempt it first as we cannot guarantee the success of the charm having never used it ourselves. A better use for an aardvark, given its average weight of 80–150 lb and length of up to 7 feet, is to freeze it solid and use it as a bludgeoning weapon.

ABYSS

An abyss, as described in the Collins dictionary, is *a very deep hole or chasm*, and you most certainly wouldn't want to end up in one of those during the days of the dead. Abyss, however, is also a very atmospheric word that can be used when you wish to come across as a mean and moody person of action when implementing a dangerous plan.

ALIENS

I know exactly what you're planning to do – you're planning to skip this bit because you think it's a bit silly to be discussing aliens in a book that purports to be about zombies. Well, I'm afraid if you want to learn all there is to learn you're just going to have to suck it up and carry on reading as aliens may very well be an issue.

It is a distinct possibility that, should aliens exist, they may have the technology and capability of reanimating the dead and giving them a penchant for biting and shambling. We have chemical weapons of our own so it's within the realms of possibility that aliens may invade our planet by turning our dead against us. They could also come along and take over our bodies like in *Invasion of the Body Snatchers* (the original and not the wishy-washy Nicole Kidman remake. Didn't you just want her to stop whining about her kid and shoot Daniel Craig in the head?). Thus they could create parasitic zombies (see **Classification: Parasitic Zombie**). It is also mildly plausible that a zombie apocalypse could be caused accidentally on their part (we're managing to destroy our own planet by a series of industrial 'accidents' so it's no great leap to think an alien species couldn't do the same).

These theories are, of course, conjecture. As yet, there is no definitive proof that there is any life out there in the vast glory of space other than this one little planet just spinning around trying to make something of itself. It would, however, be rather self-indulgent of us to assume that we are the only intelligent life form to exist in the universe, either by God's design or by evolutionary process (whichever your favourite cheese happens to be), which may lead you to wonder why, if they are 'out there', have they not bothered to show themselves yet?

Scholars will say that it is because we are at heart a violent race and are intent on our own destruction, so intelligent life from far-off planets would not dream of coming here for fear of being captured, experimented on or infected by our dirty human genes. I have my own personal theory on why aliens have decided to steer clear and that is that in September 1977 the Carpenters released the song 'Calling Occupants of Interplanetary Craft'. Anyone passing by in their spaceship and hearing those lyrics blasted over the airwaves would have serious second thoughts about visiting a planet that beseeched the 'interstellar policeman' to give us a sign we've reached him. They would just wind up their windows and fly on by, warning the kids in the back seat never to get mixed up with the weirdos on that planet.

FACT 1: The British have a long-standing joke about folks from America being a bit kooky and 'out there'. So would any Brits care to explain why this song only charted at number 31 in the US charts whilst you took it all the way to number 9? (And you Irish have nothing to laugh about! It reached number 1 in your charts!)

FACT 2: To stop any nerdy nerdy geek geeks writing in, I am fully aware the original was released by Klaatu in 1976 but they were a progressive rock band who named themselves after the alien from *The Day the Earth Stood Still* so you expect them to be a little 'out there'. The Carpenters sang Burt Bacharach lyrics and Sesame Street songs, what on earth are they doing trying to contact aliens? Did I just answer my own question then?

ALLERGIES

When a person becomes a zombie, they will still bear the physical characteristics from when they were alive (i.e. they'll still have blue eyes, a large nose, ginger hair – god forbid). They will also carry over any physical ailments, meaning that if they were in a wheelchair when they were alive, they would still be unable to walk as a zombie. Deductive reasoning should lead us to believe that if a person was allergic to something when they were alive, they will be allergic to it when they become a member of Team Z. If we are to subscribe to this theory then the best weapon to carry around with you is a peanut.

Approximately 798,188 people are allergic to peanuts in the UK (that's about the population of Leeds… Or two Manchesters… Four Portsmouths or 40 Bangors). In a worst-case scenario this allergy can cause anaphylactic shock or even death. So laying peanuts around the outside of your safehouse should act as a reasonable deterrent.

Unfortunately, as everything but zombies' brains shut down and it tends to be the respiratory system that is affected by anapphalacticaicalaphan…(these long medical words escape me, but you get the drift), this may not actually work. But, if it doesn't, you could still try throwing the peanuts really hard and hope to pierce an attacking zombie's skull. Or if you had a lot of peanuts you could drop them on the zombie, thus crushing him. Or if you dropped a peanut from the top of the Empire State building it could reach the velocity of a bullet and smash the zombie's brain… Or you could just use an axe.

ALTRUISM

Ah, good. I was hoping that there would be an A word that would cover this subject of selflessness and helping others. That way I wouldn't have to wait too long before teaching you the best way to behave during a zombie apocalypse – being altruistic isn't it.

When the undead rise you must become the most selfish, self-absorbed, egotistical person EVER. Survival (and this may come as a shock to some of you) is about *surviving* and you're only going to do that if you completely and unequivocally look after number one. And if I need to make this any clearer – the number one I am talking about is YOU.

1) Do not give your food away to anyone unless you are getting something useful in return – even if they are dying of hunger. By giving your supplies to them you only delay the inevitable death of both of you.

2) Do not give your weapons away to anyone unless you get something useful in return. You will learn from this book that anything can be utilised as a weapon so if someone is useless enough to have found nothing to use as a weapon it will be a waste of time giving them your valuable items.

3) Do not let anyone into your safe house – even if you know, love and cherish them. Who's to say they haven't been bitten or infected? Even a loved one will lie to you in order to aid their own survival.

4) Lie, cheat and steal to get what you want. Even consider murder as a viable option. As the apocalypse rages on, resources will become scarcer and it will

become a dog-eat-dog world. Make sure you are the
biggest dog in the kennel otherwise you will be left
with nothing.

This may all seem a little harsh and if you are a mild-mannered person of essentially quite a British upbringing it will be a difficult adjustment. Trust me, though. If you do not adopt this attitude you will fail in your quest for survival. You will learn to live with the guilt.

ANIMALS

One of the most frequently asked questions by anyone attending my seminars is 'Dr Dale, can I have your telephone number?', the answer to which greatly depends on how attractive and affluent the questioner is.

One of the second most frequently asked questions is 'Can animals become zombies?' As we have yet to experience the apocalypse, and so are unaware of what form of outbreak we will encounter, it would be remiss of me to give a definitive answer.

However, research at the School of Survival states that it would be highly unlikely for us to come face to face with a zombie hamster (not only because hamsters are so small and would have to be perched on a bookcase, or a child's head, in order to come face to face with you).

The deductive reasoning behind this is as follows: *The most likely cause of a zombie outbreak is through experimentation gone wrong. The experimentation would have to be carried out on humans in order to be transmitted to humans in order to create a zombie apocalypse. The fact that the experiment was so complex that it could reanimate a human corpse and could only be destroyed by eliminating the brain would mean that it would be a very specific experiment unlikely to cross-pollinate to other species with different genetic make-up and biology. Ergo, the zombie virus would not transmit to animals.*

Of course, science is never an exact science and you may be thinking that if diseases like swine flu, bird flu and mad cow disease can pass from animals to humans, then it's safe to assume that no matter how specific the disease, it could still mutate and transfer from humans to animals. To further substantiate that particular theory, we have had some small success in the School of Survival in proving that animals will suffer from human diseases, and thus far have managed to give a goldfish Alzheimer's, a duck chickenpox, a chicken duckpox and a kangaroo gonorrhoea.

Bear in mind that both humans and animals can be equally affected by rabies, which is the closest to a zombie virus. In fact, humans may not become infected at all and we may instead be faced with a kitten apocalypse, which does not bear thinking about. Come to think of it, your best bet on hearing of a zombie outbreak, is to kill all nearby animals immediately – including beloved family pets – and put them in cold storage to be used later for food. It's always better to be safe than sorry.

ANIMALS (TRAINING OF)

Should it transpire that animals are immune to the zombie virus, and you didn't follow my advice of immediately placing them in cold storage due to a misguided sentimental attachment to your gerbil Puffin, you could always consider *training* animals to help you during the zombie apocalypse.

Animals can be taught to carry out any number of simple tasks: going on scavenging missions, search and rescue, attack and defence, diversion, guarding safe houses or carrying supplies. The first animal that springs to mind when considering likely animals to train is, of course, a dog.

However, even though they are probably the most domesticated and easily trained of animals, this does not necessarily make dogs the best option. Historically, dogs and humans have a strong emotional bond, some people even value the companionship of our four-legged friends over that of other humans – they dress them up in little outfits and put bows on their ears and carry them around in purpose-made handbags and make videos of them doing cute things like falling down stairs or chasing their own tails and then send the tapes to *You've Been Framed* giving ITV a reason to keep showing the programme and torturing the rest of humanity... My point (apart from that people who do that should be stabbed with a pointy stick) is that humans can become easily attached to dogs and would be unlikely to send their beloved canine companions out to battle with a horde of zombies unprotected.

Where does that leave us? Taking this emotional weakness into consideration, and after many hours of research, we have discovered that in actual fact the best animals to train up are sheep.

The good thing about sheep is that there are lots of them and they all look alike. They are docile and easily led and can be trained to carry out simple tasks. Scientists can also clone sheep. So if you run out of natural sheep you can just nip along to your local cloning centre and get some more. The mere fact that they all look alike means that if you have several highly trained sheep on your team you will be unable to tell them apart and therefore will not become emotionally attached to them (unless you put different coloured hats on each of the sheep, but bear in mind that whilst you are not looking the sheep may swap hats meaning that you may still be uncertain of which sheep is which. They're crafty like that, are sheep).

The only thing to consider when training sheep is that they are not very good at multitasking and so you will only be able to train each sheep to carry out one specific task. These tasks are as follows:

Attack Sheep:
A sheep that will attack. Sheep aren't particularly good at jumping so their attacks will be focused mainly on areas of the zombie below the knee level. It is possible to train the sheep to lever itself on its hind legs against the zombie, therefore raising its mouth to chest level, but this still won't take it to the level of the brain. You can only hope that the zombie will stoop low to fight back, thus putting its head in the line of fire. Either that or you could train the sheep to stand on top of each other.

Defence Sheep:
Sheep can be trained to form natural barriers against doors and windows and can cause enough ballast (depending on the number of sheep) to hold a door or window closed, or block a passageway or street. You can also use defence sheep whilst

travelling from place to place. If you stand in the centre of a group of sheep, the zombies will attack them first leaving you time to escape while the undead chomp on your woolly friends.

Reconnaissance Sheep:

A sheep can blend into most surroundings as long as it is covered in snow or clouds. If this is the case then you can send a sheep to carry out reconnaissance work by strapping a video camera to its back. As it cannot be seen, it will be able to return to you unscathed.

Guard Sheep:

The piercing 'Baa' of a sheep could raise the dead. But it's not raising the dead you're worried about, it's drawing attention to yourself from the undead.

Sheep are always alert. They may fool onlookers by seeming docile and stupid, but secretly those piercing eyes are watching every movement like a hawk. A sheep can also be trained to recognise your friends as well as your enemies, and can be placed as an effective sentry on a door as long as the password is 'Baa'.

Search Sheep:

This is the one area of difficulty we have encountered in effectively training sheep. More often than not when sent on a search mission to find supplies, they will invariably lead us to grass. Be prepared to put time and effort into training the search sheep. Unless you like grass.

Of course, sheep are not the only animals that can be trained to carry out these tasks. These creatures have also shown themselves to be suitable for training: cows, pigs, ducks, badgers, frogs and voles. Just ensure that should you run out of sheep and have to use a different animal for sentry duty, you make your team aware that the password is no longer 'Baa' to avoid unnecessary confusion.

ANORAK

NO! NO! NO! They are brightly coloured so you will be easily spotted, and they rustle so you will be heard from a million miles away. OK, so they're waterproof, but I can assure you that in these dire circumstances rain will be the least of your worries. The only advantage to your wearing an anorak is that when you become a zombie (which you will because your friends will happily sacrifice you) it will be twice as enjoyable to kill you.

ANTHRACITE

Anthracite coal is probably the best fuel to use during a zombie apocalypse. Not only does it burn with little smoke or flame – so will be less likely to attract attention – but it also gives off intense heat and lasts longer than normal coal. The only downside to using this particular form of fuel is that it is very difficult to come by. Your best bet to actually obtain this special and rare item is to find an anthracite mine and to make that your command post and sanctuary during the siege of the dead.

A plus point to setting up your base in an anthracite mine is that in its very nature a mine is underground (apart from cloud mines) and thus will have limited access points for zombies to get in – and these are easily guarded. The problem is that there are very few anthracite mines around. The most famous of all the anthracite mines is based in Pottsville, Pennsylvania, and although this may seem like a bit of a trek for some of you, we do recommend you make the effort to get to it. Not only does it have an anthracite mine, but it is also built on top of seven hills (making it easier to fortify). The population is also very low, currently estimated at under 15,000, so there'd be fewer zombies to kill if they become infected.

I think this advice is best summed up in the words of General James Nagle: 'In times of the rising of corpses, head for the Pottsville anthracite mine in Pennsylvania.'

Wise words indeed.

ARMOUR (MEDIEVAL)

Do not bother wearing a suit of armour. It will be heavy and unwieldy. It will greatly reduce your speed and most importantly is an absolute nightmare to remove when you need a wee.

ARMOUR (OTHER TYPES)

Although you should definitely avoid wearing medieval armour, as explained in the previous entry, there are other forms of protective clothing that you may also have considered. Riot gear for example, or martial arts training gear, or indeed a shark suit (being a suit that protects against shark bites rather than a suit that makes you look like a shark). I'm not saying that it's not a good idea to wear armour if you have it to hand but I wouldn't go out of my way to seek it out as protective clothing.

In order to survive, you need to avoid the undead and surely preparing to be bitten is tempting fate somewhat? Thinking you are completely protected from zombie bites will give you a false sense of security and you may put yourself in more dangerous situations. One minute you're strolling down the road and the zombies appear. You don't run, you think you can walk straight through the horde, but then more and more of them appear and you decide this wasn't such a good idea after all so you jump into the nearby river to escape, but there's a shark in there and it attacks you but it can't bite through the shark suit and it gets annoyed and swims off and you think you're safe, but you're not because the shark just went to get its mate – the Mega Shark – and then the Giant Octopus turns up too and now you're truly screwed.

See what happens when you tempt fate by wearing armour? Take my advice and concentrate on avoidance rather than protection – it'll make life easier.

ATTORNEY

Also referred to as a solicitor or lawyer. An attorney will not be terribly useful during an apocalypse (although if mine survives he assures me that he has found a legal loophole that will grant me ownership of Devon should all the inhabitants die).

You should, however, keep an attorney on retainer while you are training for the apocalypse. They may prove useful when that stray throwing star hits an old lady in the head, or you accidentally knock a post office down with a rickshaw. They will keep you out of prison and quash any fines, leaving you to continue your preparation.

AUTHORITIES

From all the research we have done into how people within positions of power and authority will react during a zombie apocalypse, we have garnered one singularly important piece of information: they will be of no help at all. Their complete ineptitude, ignorance and failure to accept the seriousness of the situation before it's too late will no doubt lead to hundreds of thousands dying and being reanimated. So our advice is to not bother going anywhere near any person in a position of power, because you will end up dead.

Councils and Governments will nod sagely and tell us that everything is under control even when their offices are overrun and their secretaries are being gnawed on by the undead.

What do they have to worry about? They've got their own secret bunkers to dive into. And they probably started the whole thing anyway by sanctioning some deranged scientific experiment.

The Army will follow protocol to the letter. Trusting that their superiors know what's going on they will quarantine infected areas leaving those who have not yet been bitten unable to escape. They will pay no attention to anyone who is trying to explain to them that their whole family has just been infected, and they will happily nuke entire cities just to keep the infection under control, with no regard for anyone who may still be alive inside. After all, what's a little collateral damage between friends?

What do they have to worry about? They've got guns as standard issue. And they probably started the whole thing anyway through some deranged weapons experiment.

29

The Police will pat you on the head and tell you to run along home now, sonny, when you try and explain to them that the local shopping centre has been invaded by the undead. On subsequently learning the truth, they will incarcerate you and hold you to blame. They will immediately instigate martial law and kill anything that vaguely resembles a zombie. We are led to believe this is due to fear and panic, but really it's because deep down they're all power-crazed maniacs who are all fully paid-up members of the local fascist society.

They will pay no attention to anyone else's advice and invariably get themselves killed en masse due to badly organised strike teams. They will most definitely set up a road block somewhere that consists of two police vehicles placed in a chevron formation and then hide behind their bonnets with a megaphone (one or both of these police vehicles will then subsequently explode).

What do they have to worry about? They've got the law on their hands. And they probably started the whole thing anyway by failing to spot and control the initial outbreak.

Secret Government and Non-Government Organisations will stay very much out of the way. They won't even leave their office or secret laboratory. Ever. They will attempt to aid the other authorities by feeding them irrelevant information so that they don't get the blame for the mass carnage that is occurring. They will be searching continually for a cure to the infection and will always be so close but so far.

What do they have to worry about? They have endless funding and resources and are securely locked away in their high-security offices. And they probably started the whole thing anyway, that being the kind of thing secret organisations do.

The Women's Institute will call a meeting immediately to attempt to reschedule the jams and jellies social to a time when Marjorie isn't chomping on her husband. They will try to find an alternative venue for the summer fête as the field they had planned to use is now overrun with the undead. They will realise that raffle prizes will now become more difficult to come by as shops are being looted by scavengers, and although they know that they will have to cancel their coach trip to Bognor, they will come up with an alternative social event to keep their members happy.

What do they have to worry about anyway? They probably started the whole thing…or perhaps not. Who knows though?

FACT 1: Though we have made it perfectly clear that the authorities as a whole are not to be trusted during an apocalypse, there is usually one member of each group who is plucky, courageous and willing to help (they're usually new to the department so haven't had time to be poisoned with cynicism and machismo). If you must go to the authorities try and link up with this one person.

FACT 2: All research regarding the authorities' reaction to the rising of the dead has been taken from varying filmic sources and is probably in no way connected to how they will react in real life. For all we know they already have a secret zombie plan that will save us all when the dead rise – but how can I comment on that if they insist on keeping it a secret? If they just told us the truth now and then and were a little bit more transparent then maybe they wouldn't be depicted as Hitlerian egomaniacs or shambling goons in every zombie film that has ever been made.

BACTERIA

In 1998 an American scientist calculated that the number of bacteria on earth was 5,000,000,000,000,000,000,000,000,000,000. One can assume from this man's findings that:

a) in over ten years this figure has increased and

b) this man never got much sex.

So, how will this very long number affect us when attempting to survive a zombie apocalypse? Bacteria will be both our best friend and possibly our worst enemy during these dark times.

There are good bacteria and there are bad bacteria (for proof of this, speak to Mr Yakult). Unfortunately, we are more likely to encounter the bad bacteria (the likes of which cause tetanus, typhoid fever, diphtheria, syphilis, cholera, food-borne illness, leprosy, tuberculosis and other life-threatening illnesses) than the good bacteria (like Lactobacillus and Lactococcus that make cheese).

With society on its knees, medicines are going to become scarce so we will be more susceptible. There is not much you can do about this other than to take simple precautions such as: ensuring you and your sanctuary are kept clean; if you do suffer injuries, attempt to sterilise them; and if food begins to spoil get rid of it. Should you, however, discover a way in which to destroy all bacteria I implore you – DON'T. Bacteria is also our greatest natural asset in the war against zombies. It is bacteria that makes them rot.

Although this may seem like a rather time-consuming way to defeat the undead, bear in mind that given the right conditions (hotter climate) and with the help of insects, a human body can rot away to just bone in anywhere between 50 and 365 days.

So, with the help of bacteria, it will all just be a case of bedding down and waiting for our inevitable victory! With a wine and cheese celebration afterwards.

BALD

This is the best way to present one's head during a zombie apocalypse – and quite possibly the rest of your body too should you be a rather hirsute person. The reasoning behind this has less to do with fashion and more to do with giving a zombie as little as possible to grab on to should you be attacked. Zombies are known to fight like girls and will grab your hair, bite and quite possibly pinch you too if they have the chance.

Having no hair will also make you a faster swimmer – according to the Goodhew theory of aerodynamics.

BARRICADES

A barricade is what is needed when a door just won't do the job on its own. If you have a large number of zombies to keep out then you need to pile as much stuff as possible in front of all the access points to make it as difficult as possible for them to get in. Furniture is the preferred item for use in a barricade.

Those of you who regularly watch TV will note that in situations when a barricade is needed, there is usually a well-placed chest of drawers or cabinet next to the door or window that needs blocking. Don't rely on one being there when you need it. If you have decided to make an ultra-modern apartment building your sanctuary you might have noticed that the minimalist attitude of the previous tenants leaves you with very little furniture. This is where your inventiveness will have to come into play and you may be forced to use alternative items to create a barricade (e.g. books, clothes, fish – if the previous tenant had an aquarium). As long as you have enough of something, it will make an effective enough barricade.

Be aware that a barricade does not have to be placed in front of a door or window – you can also pile items onto stairs, making upper floors inaccessible, and down corridors, essentially blocking off segments of your safe house.

KEEPING YOUR BARRIER SAFE

1) As well as being effective at keeping zombies out, be aware that your barricade should also be easy to dismantle in case you need to get out of your safe house quickly.

2) Never build a personal barricade by constructing four walls of furniture completely around yourself with a roof on top. Other survivors may mistake it for an unlit bonfire and then you will be in the same situation as hedgehogs on bonfire night.

BIRDS

Birds are around so much that in normal everyday life we rarely notice them. During an apocalypse, though, it is worth keeping an eye out for our feathered friends as they can tell us much about how safe an area is.

It is worth noting that evidence suggests zombies will attack any living creature. So we will presume that birds are also viable prey for the undead.

Pigeon

Pigeons are generally found living in urban areas and are known as the rodents of the bird world due to their habit of scavenging. They are also very intelligent and will become aware that zombies are a danger to them. You can therefore use them as an advance warning system. If you see a flock of pigeons suddenly take to the skies, then you can be assured that something has disturbed them and you can keep away from that area of town. The downside to this is that if a flock of pigeons was in that area, there was probably something worth eating. Make your choice! Stay or go – but the pigeons warned you.

Crow

Like any carrion-eating bird, if you see a flock hovering about you can be certain there's something dead below – and the more crows, the more dead things. It is true that, like pigeons, these creatures will show caution once they realise it is dangerous to attack zombies, but they are also brave and will devise tactics to pick off the flesh without being caught. This is how you will know that the dead meat they are after is still alive. If it weren't a threat, they wouldn't be hovering, they'd be down there eating it. Be warned, though. Once crows realise that zombies are tasty pickings, they may attack the living too, as they will not be able to differentiate between the two. And being attacked by birds isn't nice – just ask Tippi Hedren.

Ostrich

Contrary to popular belief, ostriches do not bury their heads in the ground when faced with danger; rather, they lie their necks flat and lower their bodies so they blend into the landscape and look like mounds of earth. This is actually quite clever so let's immediately stop with the ridiculing of the humble ostrich and begin paying this bird some respect. With a top speed of 45 mph (the fastest bird on land) and with a lethal kick, the ostrich is a good role model to have.

Flamingo

The Queen of Hearts used one as a croquet mallet, which is a good enough reason as any to use a flamingo as a battering weapon. If a fictional character from a children's story book can do it then by golly so can you.

Chicken

Of course this bird is useful! They lay eggs which will sustain you if you can capture one and keep it in your safe house. If all else fails you can also eat it. In fact, you could eat any bird at all if it's cooked properly, although a chicken will make a more substantial meal than a budgie. The largest bird is the ostrich, but he is a god amongst birds so you wouldn't want to anger the god of ostrich by eating him. After the ostrich I suppose the next best thing is Big Bird of *Sesame Street*. You'd need a lot of Tupperware boxes to keep the leftovers after cooking him!

BITES

If you are bitten by a zombie you can do one of two things: either kill yourself by destroying your own brain, or let someone else kill you using the same brain-destroying method. DO NOT ignore the fact you have been bitten and hope it will go away. It won't. Eventually, you will become a zombie, making survival more difficult for other living folks who weren't stupid enough to get bitten.

No one knows exactly how long it takes to transform once you have been bitten. Because of this it is wise to regularly make all the members of your group strip naked to check that no one is hiding anything. Take no chances either! If someone says they cut themselves shaving, assume they are lying and smash in their head immediately.

If you are alone when bitten with no plausible way of destroying your own brain, then unfortunately there is no way to stop yourself from becoming a zombie. There is, however, a way in which you can stop yourself from becoming a danger to other survivors and that is to neutralise your own head. This can be done in a variety of ways, but my preferred method is to use cling film. Wrap it multiple times around your head, and then gaffer tape it afterwards (with maybe a few staples). Then, when you do rise you will be unable to bite other survivors. Other methods of head neutralisation include visored motorcycle helmets, heavy-duty bin bags and strapping a cat to your face.

BOAT

The use of boats to aid your survival is a sensible choice – as long as you use caution and remember that zombies can survive under water and withstand strong currents.

Let us look at some of the options you have:

Battleship
Built to withstand heavy weather conditions and contains weapons and supplies. Be aware that it is not constructed for comfort and fuel will be hard to come by. The armed forces are also known for manning their ships with fine specimens of humankind, which will make it easier to repopulate when the time comes.

Rowing boat
If your safe house is near a river or canal it is always handy to have a rowboat as a means of escape across the water should the need arise. However, we would not recommend living in one, especially if there is a team of more than 47 in your group, as it may get a little cramped and water-bound zombies can easily overpower a rowboat and capsize it.

Cruise liner
These boats are great if you can find one that isn't already swarming with zombies – but due to the fact they are *public* liners that is unlikely. But if you do manage to secure one, as long as it is well stocked and kept off shore, these are the best boats to live on – as long as you don't mind playing bingo every night from 5–7p.m.

Pirate ship

Not the most substantial vessel to attempt long-term survival on the choppy ocean waves, but it is certainly the coolest. It will also give you the right to cease washing and braid your hair. You can also sing sea shanties about yourself and catch scurvy, none of which will really help in surviving a zombie apocalypse.

Peddle-mechanism swan boat

No.

BOTOX

Want to stay looking calm during a zombie apocalypse? That furrowed brow and those worry lines starting to affect your team's confidence in you? Is constantly fighting the undead taking its toll? Worry no more as Botox could very well be the one thing every survivalist needs in their kit. Injecting small amounts of Botox into the lined areas on your face will eradicate any signs of anxiety making you look cool, calm and collected at all times. Botox can also be used to control excessive sweating, stop facial tics, treat migraines, help bladder control, alleviate pain involved with muscle disorders, fly an aeroplane, explain the theory of relativity and make a mean gazpacho soup (the last three are currently unconfirmed but undergoing clinical trials).

USING BOTOX ON ZOMBIES

The effect of Botox as a weapon against the undead cannot be commented on until we can be aware of exactly how a zombie operates physiologically and whether large doses would cause temporary or fatal paralysis of the muscles or nervous system within the brain. You can be assured, though, that studies will likely reveal that eight out of ten zombies injected with Botox will notice younger, more vibrant-looking skin.

BYPASS/BYROAD

Bypass roads are going to be extremely useful during the dark days of the apocalypse as they will be one of the safest routes to travel from A to B. No matter what mode of transport you decide to use – car, bus, motorcycle, tank, walking, boat, pram or dog with a saddle – using bypass roads will enable you to stay out of built-up areas where there are likely to be more infected people. By their very nature, bypass roads 'bypass' or 'pass by' towns and cities without actually going straight through them, and although the temptation may be quite high to enter built-up areas to scavenge for supplies, we highly recommend against it if you wish to live. Stay on bypass routes and get what you need from smaller villages and remote farms, avoiding urban areas.

It is with this in mind that the School of Survival is lobbying for more bypasses to be constructed. When the dead finally rise, a bypass will be more useful to the survival of the human race than a field, some trees and an area of natural beauty. So if a faceless construction firm, the council or the government wishes to build a bypass in your area, ignore those who are fighting against it in order to preserve the habitat of the blue-spotted toad and get that bypass built! In the end, whose survival is more important? Yours or a toad's?

CAMERA

Of course the last thing on your mind during an apocalypse is getting a spiffy new profile picture for Facebook, but a camera is useful for so much more than capturing memories to treasure for ever.

Cameras are more readily available than binoculars or telescopes, and the zoom function will aid you on your reconnaissance missions. Also, as most cameras now allow you to view pictures on a tiny screen at the back, you can spend more time analysing a situation from the safety of your base without having to rely on memory or having to find a printer. If you are on a scavenging mission and running back to your safe house, you can also hold your camera aloft and take random pictures of streets and shops as you run. Later on, you can look through the saved pictures at your leisure and identify the areas that may be worth going back to. You can also use the camera to take pictures of the more attractive members of your team during strip searches for bites. As porn will be in short supply these will come in handy on cold winter nights.

CAMOUFLAGE

The way in which a zombie perceives the world is open to debate. With them being technically dead, how do their eyes operate? Can they smell? Does their hearing become more acute? Until they rise we can do no more than speculate, but we can theorise that camouflage will be a waste of time.

The concept behind camouflage is to blend into an area that you wish to remain in for a specific purpose without being seen by your enemies. In this case your enemies are zombies. What purpose could you possibly have for being in the same room as a zombie? Why would you want to stay hidden in a room where there were zombies? If they have gained access to your safe house then the most logical course of action is not to stick a lampshade on your head and stand in a corner. Either:

1) Run away.
2) Try and fight them off.
3) Hide.

Hiding is not to be confused with camouflage. Hiding is secreting yourself in an attic and making no noise so as not to be seen. Camouflage is painting yourself the same colour as the wallpaper and standing flat against the wall in plain sight of intruders. With a zombie's brain being the only functioning organ, you can pretty much guarantee that they're not going to be stupid enough to miss a plonker who has painted himself purple and is standing by the telly.

CAR

Cars, much like chainsaws, have a major stumbling block in that they require fuel, a commodity that will be in short supply once the apocalypse is in full swing. It is, however, advisable to try and secure a decent vehicle should the need arise for a quick escape or a long-haul trip.

In inner-city areas it is likely that the streets will be blocked with debris, bodies, sweet wrappers and other cars. Therefore, using a motor vehicle in these areas will be near impossible (unless you attach a lot of pigeons to the roof rack and airlift the car out). However, should your safe house be in a city, it is always a good idea to secure the keys to vehicles that are situated in your scavenging zones. This way, should you come under surprise attack you will have a possible means of escape or a place in which to hide until a rescue party arrives. Do be careful when searching vehicles for keys or supplies; there will be cases where people have been attacked whilst in their cars and will have turned into zombies whilst stuck inside. As zombies won't know how to operate seatbelts or car doors, they may still be trapped inside. This is even more likely where children are concerned as adult zombies may have the brute strength to break free, whereas a child zombie strapped in a car seat may not.

CELEBRITY

As horrible and upsetting as it may sound, celebrities can also become zombies. In fact, anyone can become a zombie and although we've all pretty much come to terms with the fact that your own mum may be reanimated, are we fully conditioned to accept an undead Richard and Judy, a zombie Philip Schofield or a feral Fearne Cotton? And, as amusing as it may sound, celebrity zombies can be a dangerous thing.

If a well-known A-List celebrity like Britney Spears so much as sneezes these days there are numerous photographers on hand to snap the event and ten times as many fans ready to set up a Facebook group to say 'Geshundheit'.

Imagine, then, if Britney were to be bitten and transformed? Initially *Heat* magazine would comment on her weight loss and deathly pallor, maybe coming to the conclusion that she had been in rehab. But once the full truth of the situation dawned on the populace there would be those crazed fans out there who would want to either a) try and save her – even though we all know that once reanimated you are beyond help, or b) own her.

If a celebrity becomes a mindless corpse, crazed and opportunistic fans are likely to relish the chance of being able to own their idol, causing a mass of people to congregate at her last known location giving little thought to their own safety or the possibility that their beloved Britney will most likely attack them. This will result in a higher level of zombies in otherwise deserted and exclusive areas like Primrose Hill, Notting Hill and Beverley Hills. (It seems to be that wherever there is a Hill you'll find a celebrity – apart from maybe an ant hill. You'll only find ants there, and not the kind who hangs around with Dec – the insecty type... I digress).

Another problem for celebrities is that they may be mistaken for the actual characters they play in movies and other media, and might be expected to perform acts of immense courage, strength and near impossibility in order to help us survive. So although Woody Harrelson, Bruce Campbell or Milla Jovovich may be able to hold their own quite well during the apocalypse due to the previous simulation training they've had in their day jobs, it would be unwise to expect them to be able to make bus tanks, clone themselves or mix magic health potions from cabbage and pies. Just concentrate on your own survival and don't worry about the celebrities at all. Just remember, once you've got through this, you'll be the celebrity for using your knowledge to help the needy survive!

> **NOTE:** For those who take umbrage at my use of Britney Spears as an example during this segment, I did initially plan to use Paris Hilton, but then realised the analogy of her transforming into a mindless corpse would have confused the issue and thus become a moot point.

CEMETERY

It is a common misconception that cemeteries and graveyards are unsafe during a zombie apocalypse. On the contrary, they are one of the safest places to be – during the initial outbreak at least. Bear in mind that the most dangerous places to be are those that are heavily populated and on the surface appear to be the most obvious areas of escape or aid (e.g. hospitals and airports - see **Panic Zones**). Who in their right mind would go to a cemetery on hearing of a zombie uprising? A cemetery will be relatively quiet with fewer members of the public to cause mass infection.

But what if the dead rise from their graves? Since 1980 the number of burials has decreased rapidly with people preferring cremation, which is cheaper and requires less space. So, luckily for you the majority of the corpses in most cemeteries have been underground for decades. And if their brains haven't already rotted away, they will still have to break through a coffin and six feet of earth to get out. As they are scrabbling up to the surface you will have enough time to dispose of them.

Your only issue may be if there is a chapel in the cemetery with bodies awaiting burial/cremation, but they can be swiftly dealt with if you are adept enough. We do not recommend using a cemetery as a long-term safe area (due to the lack of amenities, weapons and food, as well as the general atmosphere of sadness and stench of death and old people) but heading there immediately on hearing of the apocalypse will keep you safe from the initial panic and allow you to come up with a more coherent plan for your future.

CHAINSAW

Cited as the weapon of choice by 8 out of 10 zombie survivalists in the absence of any firearms, the chainsaw is indeed a fun weapon to have around when mass carnage is the task of the day. But although it is an extremely effective way to dispose of those pesky undead, and one that can also bring immense pleasure too, we would not recommend putting this particular item at the top of your Christmas list.

Firstly, your average chainsaw can weigh from 8–30 lbs making it difficult to transport along with all your other supplies.

Secondly, there is the fuel to consider. Although the blades can cause major damage when spinning around like a fairground carousel, when they *aren't* moving you may as well be hitting a zombie with a sponge. Fuel is likely to become scarce during the apocalypse and even if you do find some, carrying it around would be heavy and cumbersome.

Finally, there is the operational aspect of the trusty chainsaw.

It may look easy to use but just Google 'chainsaw death' and you'll see how many people have fallen foul of the teeth of one of these beasts – and they can't all be inbred retards. Therefore, unless you are already versed in the art of chainsaw usage, it would be a bad idea to just wade into battle waving one around your head – and do you really want to waste fuel practising at home?

Of course, here at the School of Survival we don't like to rain on anyone's parade and as using a chainsaw to chop up a ghoul can be spiffing entertainment, we advocate the use of this particular weapon in a 'defence situation' only. Once you have found and fortified your safe house, keep a chainsaw handily stored in case zombies get in. Just choose a smaller, more manageable weapon whilst out in the field.

CLASSIFICATION

As discussed in the *Introduction*, there are four distinct classes of zombies. These are each broken down into further subclasses and then broken down into even more subclasses. In fact, ultimately there are so many different classes and subclasses of zombies that you could fill a whole book with them (which incidentally will be coming soon entitled *Dr Dale's Classes, Subclasses and Sub-subclasses of Zombies – a Whole Book Full of Them*). But for now we will deal with the four main classes just to keep it simple.

Supernatural Zombie

Created by: Death

Points of interest: The apocalypse that starts for no apparent reason! And quite possibly the worst kind of zombie apocalypse to be caught in as it will never end. It's not just the bites that cause reanimation – every single person who dies will eventually reanimate. Whether they were hit by a bus, fell out of a window, accidentally stabbed themselves in the eye with a spoon whilst eating breakfast or got knocked by a bus out of a window face down onto a spoon, they will come back as zombies.

Even those who die of natural causes will ultimately reanimate – which means if you have a 21-gun salute at your funeral it would be wise for the mourners to aim the barrel directly at your head.

Genetic Zombie

Created by: A genetic mutation causes death and reanimation in the host human due to radiation, experimentation, weird gas or space dust. Will only affect the living and not the previously dead as the mutation should only occur in living cells, so no need to worry about Great-great-great Uncle Roger clawing his way out of his grave.

Points of interest: Generally speaking most zombies will look like your normal everyday walking dead human as the genetic mutations will have occurred to the organs inside the body (most likely the brain). But, in the case of Genetic zombies, the 'super-powered' zombie although unlikely, cannot be discounted. In this scenario the genetic mutation causes the zombie to become super-powered, psychokinetic, large, almost invincible and mutated.

This is a less likely eventuality but one you should still allow for in your training as we cannot completely discount the idea that we may come face to face with a big, round zombie that explodes bile all over the place when you shoot it. Or a huge, leather, S&M-clad behemoth who grunts the word 'Stars' at opportune moments just to warn you he's coming. If you were to come up against him then throw this book away and go and find a very big gun.

Parasitic Zombie

Created by: An external host takes over the body of the human, kills them, and uses their body to sate the creature's blood lust. Can affect both the living and the previously dead as the parasite is only operating the body like a puppet – like Rod Hull used Emu – although Emu didn't try and kill you...much.

Points of interest: There are two different kinds of parasite: the first will conceal itself inside the body of the human and will be unseen; the second will attach itself to the outside of the body – generally somewhere on the spine or on top of the head like a jaunty hat. The reason the headshot is important in this case is that the brain will be what the parasite needs to control the body. This does not necessarily mean that the parasite will die immediately when the brain is destroyed so you will need to be extra vigilant in looking for bloodthirsty little parasites running around trying to find a new host.

It also means you'll have to find a way to kill them too. (I can't help you with that one. This is the *Zombie Dictionary* – not the *Parasite Dictionary*. Try stamping on them or using salt – it works on slugs.)

Viral Zombie

Created by: A virus – the clue is somewhat in the name (the infection can also be bacterial, but it seems pedantic to have two separate classifications for what is essentially the same thing).

Points of interest: Probably the most likely cause of the apocalypse – the virus will attack the human immune system shutting down all internal organs until only the brain is operating on a primal blood lust. On the plus side, like the genetic zombie, the virus will only affect the living, but on the down side it is likely that the virus will not just be transmitted by bites – it may be airborne or caught by touching someone who is infected. Back to the plus side again, though – there may be those who are naturally immune – but once more to the negative – they could still be carriers and infect other non-immune living who will eventually get on a helicopter to Europe and infect Paris with the zombie plague. Hmmmm – that turned into a positive again.

CLOTHING

I have never pretended to be any sort of fashion guru – even though I have been asked on numerous occasions for advice on what's hot and what's not – but as a rule of thumb I would categorically state 'If it ain't clashin, it's not fashion'. So bear that in mind when next perusing the racks at your local Primark. However, I do have some advice on what to wear during a zombie apocalypse:

Go tight

The tighter fitting the clothes are, the better. This will give the undead less to grab onto should you be stuck in a 'hand-to-hand' situation. The best possible option is a wet-look unitard as the slippery surface will also ensure that you are able to slide, snakelike, from the grasp of any clawing hands.

Neutral colours

A zombie's perception and peripheral vision is likely to operate in much the same way as it did when they were alive. It is also wise to remember that although the undead may have heightened predatory senses we shouldn't imbue them with a supernatural sixth sense that they are unlikely to possess. It is therefore recommended that you wear unobtrusive colours that are less likely to be spotted should you have to hide quickly: darker colours at night, urban colours during the day, pastels in the spring, browns and beiges in the autumn months.

This choice of colour also works for protecting yourself from other survivors who will be able to spot you in a retro Eighties neon pink tank top from several miles away. They'll have shot that crossbow bolt into your head before you get anywhere close enough to let them know you are not a zombie.

Remember what your mum said

Always make sure you're wearing clean underwear – you may get hit by a bus. And although I always thought my mother was a little bit twisted for saying this (my grandfather was killed by a herd of stampeding buses) she was ultimately right. Buses aren't the issue here, though. It is the zombie plague that we are dealing with and should you die, it is highly likely you will rise again (unless you have very good friends – see **Euthanasia**) and I very much doubt that the first thing that enters a person's mind on seeing a zombie is 'I wonder if they have clean pants on'.

However, you must ensure that the basics of hygiene are followed in order for you to attract the best mates when it is time to repopulate the world, and wearing undergarments that are solid enough to crush a zombie's skull is not the best way to go about attracting a perfect mate.

I know you're thinking that water will be sparse and it will be difficult to wash yourself, let alone your clothing, but that is no excuse. In every populated area you encounter there will be homes and stores with a surplus of clothing so you will be able to change on a regular basis. Even if you are overly fond of your Iron Maiden tour crop top you are going to have to let it go eventually.

Don't be stupid

There are two polar opposite trains of thought in the clothing debate that are both as stupid as each other and should be disregarded without a second thought.

The first one is to wear as many clothes as possible, thus forming a protective layer of fabric around yourself to make it harder for zombies to bite through. Is it really logical to think that a zombie that can bite through gristle and flesh will be halted in its tracks by a few layers of thick-knit wool? If you are going to allow a zombie to get close enough to bite you, then he will bite you no matter what you are wearing. And I doubt very much you will be able to move quickly enough to run away or attack him in six jumpers, two hoodies, nine T-shirts, a swimsuit, three pairs of dungarees and a duffle coat.

The second of these ridiculous theories is to be completely naked. The theory is that by wearing nothing you will give your attacker nothing to grab onto. Firstly, I'm sure the men reading this can see the potential element for risk in this plan, and secondly, it's all well and good being naked in the confines of your own home whilst you're doing the ironing and *Coronation Street* is on TV but this is a zombie apocalypse we're talking about here! You may have to run for your life at any minute through streets littered with rubble and glass and people's entrails and drawing pins. It's just not practical! And don't even get me started on those people who also advocate covering themselves with a layer of grease so it's harder for the zombies to grab onto...

COCONUT

A coconut is not a particularly effective weapon to use against the undead, but with the correct application it will do the trick of destroying a brain. There is, however, an even better use for this humble nut and that is in your training.

A coconut is hard and cylindrical and thus very similar to a skull (in most cases it is actually thicker and harder). It's therefore an excellent gauge of how effective your bludgeoning weapons are and will allow you to measure just how much force is required to smash the coconut – and ergo a human skull – when the time comes. Having this handy item will also save you from having to practise on your friends or grandparents.

COSMIC ORDERING

Dear Cosmos,

Please could you stop the undead from rising? Destroy all the zombies that have already risen. Allow the human race to flourish again. Give me lots of money, a large mansion and a big penis and/or breasts (depending on what sex I am).

Yours gratefully,

A True Believer

Dear True Believer,

No.

Yours, Dr Dale

C/O The Cosmos

COUNSELLING (OTHERS)

During the apocalypse it won't always be just about katanas, machetes and eating toilet paper to survive; sometimes the battle will need to be fought with words and the occasional hug. Due to the immense knowledge of survival techniques that you will have garnered from these very pages you will naturally fall into a leadership position in your group and it will be your primary responsibility to protect everyone in it. And not just from the enemy outside – they will also need saving from themselves.

Not everyone will have taken the fall of civilisation as well as you, not everyone will have been able to accept the deaths of their loved ones as easily as you have and not everyone may be able to deal with the inevitable loss of daytime soaps from their lives. A survival team requires full mental focus in order to be successful, so, as well as being a soldier of mercy, you will also need to be a shoulder to cry on.

Counselling can take many different forms and I do not presume to know all the ins and outs of the human psyche, but here are two simple techniques I recommend for dealing with a mentally unbalanced member of your group to ensure that they remain on kilter and ready to fight. It's up to you which you prefer.

Listening

Sometimes, just sitting and listening to a person's problems can help them come to terms with their inner issues. All this technique requires is for you to sit (preferably with your legs crossed) and nod sagely and with understanding at the appropriate times.

PERFECTING YOUR NODDING TECHNIQUE

The correct nodding technique is the most difficult part of this particular strategy and you may wish to grab a mirror to practise. First furrow your brow slightly and let a sadness enter your eyes – now nod... No! That's too fast, slower, slower, slower – no – now that's too slow – somewhere in between... No! That's too fast again. Look, it might be better if I let you practise that on your own.

The beauty of this technique, once perfected, is that you don't ever actually have to listen to what is being said to you. Purely the act of nodding occasionally will give the illusion that you care and sometimes that's all someone needs. To know someone cares... Even if you really don't.

Cruel to be kind

The polar opposite of the 'Listening' technique. Sometimes people need a shock to the system to break them out of a cycle of maudlin thoughts. So if they come to talk to you about some minor issue (e.g. they're finding it difficult to cope with the solitude or they lost an arm during battle) just shout at them. Not in a random, Tourette's way – you need to be focused in your rant. Take this example below and adapt it to fit your own style:

'What? What are you talking about! You're worried about (insert person's minor problem) *when civilisation is over!! You're worried about* (repeat person's minor problem) *when all over the world millions are dead! When corpses are rising and killing people all you're worried about is* (repeat person's minor problem this time with utter contempt). *Do you realise how selfish and self-absorbed you sound? Now, get over yourself and let's go kill some zombies!'*

WHICH TECHNIQUE IS THE MOST EFFECTIVE?

In controlled tests we discovered that the 'Cruel' technique works a lot quicker than the 'Listening' technique. We also found that it is 29% more effective when used on old people and toddlers.

COUNSELLING (YOURSELF)

It is easily assumed that a highly trained individual like yourself will be a cold-hearted, single-minded dealer of death during the dark days of the apocalypse, and it would be wise to uphold this image to ensure that you have the full support of your teammates during any crazy missions you plan. Even so, you are only human, and there will be times when you will need to talk. There will be occasions when you feel that you are teetering on the edge of sanity with all the blood, guts, gore, death and destruction around you, but you won't want to reveal your weakness to the rest of your group. Who could you possibly trust with your fears? That's easy – the one person you can truly rely on during a zombie apocalypse is yourself. That's why you will also need to educate yourself in the art of self-counselling.

Of course, you don't want to be seen talking to yourself because people may then begin to question your sanity. So here at the School of Survival we have formulated a foolproof method of effective self-counselling.

1) Take a sock.

2) Put it on your hand.

3) Talk to the sock puppet (you'll have to do the voice of the sock too).

A self-counselling sock puppet may go something like this:

You: Hello there, do you mind if I talk to you about my problems?

Sock: Not at all.

You: What's your name?

Sock: That doesn't matter – let's talk about you.

You: I'd like to know your name, though.

Sock: It's not really important.

You: I'm not going to tell someone my problems if I don't know their name.

Sock: I think you're just trying to find a reason not to talk.

You: No I'm not.

Sock: Yes you are.

You: No I'm not.

Sock: Yes you are!

You: Of course I am! I just had to shoot my Aunt Mildred in the head because she got bitten! It's very upsetting!

Sock: It is upsetting, but I'm sure you feel better now after talking about it.

You: I had my first sexual experience with my Aunt Mildred.

Sock: OK, whoa there, you freak!

You: I feel so much better now.

A FEW KEY POINTS TO SELF-COUNSELLING:

1) Always try and use a clean sock — you wouldn't want to talk to someone who smells.

2) Never get angry with your counsellor and hit or stab him — it'll hurt you more than it hurts him.

3) In the absence of socks, other items of underwear CANNOT be used as a substitute. If people catch you talking to a bra they may lose confidence in you as a leader.

CRYONICS

Before we go into this in any great depth it is worth noting that there is a difference between cryonics and suspended animation. However, purely to save time, energy and space, I am going to cover both subjects under one heading.

In its simplest form, cryonics is the science of freezing a person so that they may be revived at some stage in the future. Although this may seem like a good way to avoid the apocalypse, there are some key points to bear in mind when considering this option. Although scientists have perfected the technique of freezing a body, they have not yet worked out how to revive one – and should the apocalypse occur I would imagine it would be quite low on their agenda to continue their research. Add to the equation the diminishing resources of humankind and chances are that once frozen you will remain a popsicle for ever.

The law also states that you are not allowed to be cryonically preserved until you are legally dead. This may seem like a perfect way to counteract the effects of a zombie bite should you be infected, but although being frozen until a cure is found may seem like a good idea, it all depends on how fast you will rise from the dead. Scientists cannot begin the procedure of freezing you until you are dead – by which point you will be a zombie. And although they may be able to cure the zombie virus, it is highly unlikely that science will have advanced so far as to cure death.

The other alternative is suspended animation. This is a procedure whereby your blood is replaced by a low-temperature fluid. Tests have been carried out on dogs as to the viability of this technique. In some cases they were successful, in others they created 'zombie dogs'. I think at this point we can see the problem with putting our trust in this particular science. If it could possibly turn you into a zombie, it really isn't much safer than staying alive and attempting to survive without the aid of nitrogen in your veins.

In conclusion, the idea of using any science that freezes your body is a bad idea – and when the apocalypse comes, Walt Disney is going to be extremely narked off.

CURE

There is no cure. Once you are bitten you become a zombie. So stop thinking there is a cure, because there isn't. Even if there is, you need to think there isn't. Because thinking there's a cure will give you hope and hope will make you weak and weakness will make you lose and losing means you die and dying means you rise and rising means you become a zombie – for which there is no cure. So stop thinking there's a cure because that will give you hope and hope will make you weak and... You get the message – THERE IS NO CURE!

CUTLERY

This is the easiest and most accessible form of weapon. Most houses, flats, apartments, shops, farms and florists boast at least one of the three basic items of cutlery. They are also small, light, easy to carry and multifunctional too (should the need arise you could even use them for eating food).

Contrary to popular belief, the most effective weapon in a cutlery set is not the knife. These can often be blunt with rounded edges (unless it is a posh cutlery set with a steak knife, but don't bank on that). If given the option of only one implement, we advise on choosing the fork. The blades will be pointier and they can also be bent and used for picking locks, prying open cupboards, cleaning fingernails and drawing three equal-spaced lines in sand.

If left with only a spoon, reverse the item and poke the handle through eye sockets for maximum effect.

OTHER USEFUL ITEMS OF CUTLERY

SPORK – spoon/fork

SPIFE – spoon/knife

KNORK – knife/fork

SPLAYD – all three

FLUDPT – don't know

One wonders if the person who invented these should not have spent their time more wisely. Perhaps by killing themselves and thus doing their family and the world a favour.

DANCE

You may be the kind of person who wants to dance with somebody, (and invariably someone who loves you) or you may really not feel like dancing at all when that old Joanna plays. Either way, dance cannot be discounted as a frivolous pastime. Look at Billy Elliot. He took up ballet and then had a major film made about him and a musical by Elton John (mind you, Julie Walters was his ballet teacher so he already had the contacts in the business to get him started). But despite the associated fame, dance is a tough occupation and dance training will most certainly be beneficial in a zombie apocalypse.

Ballet dancers go through a great deal of physical discomfort in their training. As well as being accustomed to pain, they can contort their bodies into strange and unnatural shapes and are also capable of bounding thousands of feet in a single leap (unconfirmed fact).

If you don't have the time to learn ballet yourself then it would be extremely useful to have a ballerina on your team. As well as being capable of accessing unreachable places they also eat very little so will not be a drain on your resources. Female ballet dancers are also very light and suitable for use as a throwing weapon. Both male and female ballet dancers wear very tight outfits all the time so bites will be easy to spot and the little pink-ribboned shoes they wear have wooden blocks in the toes so they could be used to kick in a zombie's head.

Ballet is not the only form of dance that can come in handy during a zombie apocalypse, so it may be worth learning the most relevant moves from each form to keep you prepared for all eventualities.

Tap dancing

The basis of this dance is to make a noise with your feet. Although under normal circumstances this would attract the undead, shoes with metal plates attached to the base will also make perfect weapons. You can either hold the shoe in your hands and strike, or if you have supple enough legs, you can wear them on your feet and kick. At any rate, they're better than a leatherette moccasin.

Street dance

Not, as some may believe, purely dancing in the streets à la Jagger and Bowie. Street dance incorporates movements specific to the beats of a given song. Often aggressive in its choreography, it is the closest dance to a form of martial arts and incorporates elbows, fists, knees and floor work which can be useful for incapacitating and avoiding foes.

For those unfamiliar with this form of dance, look out for it in modern hip hop music videos – which is ironic as street doesn't include an awful lot of hopping (although some hip movement is necessary).

Morris dancing
A dance that involves grown men attempting to hit each other with sticks. You may wish to dispense with the bells around your ankles, the hanky-waving segment and the skipping, but this is a dance involving *hitting things with sticks*. The value is immeasurable.

Pole dancing
There may be time during the apocalypse when the need arises for you to make a quick escape up a greased pole in a sensual manner whilst wearing hardly any clothes. This is why we fully advocate pole dancing as part of a zombie apocalypse training regime.

Line dancing
No.

DARKNESS

Not the now defunct UK rock band that boasted high-pitched vocals from frontman Justin Hawkins (he would attract too much attention). Nor the Top Cow comic book (although having the power to create anything you desire at night time would be most useful during a zombie apocalypse). The darkness I'm referring to in this entry is actual darkness – the time when there is no light.

In normal warfare, darkness is advantageous as one can use it to move around without being seen, or carry out covert attacks or operations. But in the war against the undead it is a complete hindrance.

The problem with having the undead as an enemy is that they could be anywhere – standing around aimlessly, sitting in cars, under tables, in fridges, in ponds or up trees. This means that when travelling from a to b you have to always be alert.

Darkness can affect your ability to see and therefore affect your vigilance. The use of lights and torches is a bad idea too as zombies will acclimatise to their surroundings and a moving light will attract their attention (whereas during the day, movement could be attributed to anything: other zombies, animals, curtains flapping in the wind, collapsing buildings etc., so a zombie would be less likely to react).

You could use night-time goggles, but although these are useful in some situations, they will restrict your peripheral vision.

In the darkness, zombies will head for you – whether it's through sight, smell, sound, body heat, who knows? – but they will lock onto you as a target and move in. You won't be able to see anything. You will be disorientated, lost and a sitting duck with no idea where to head for safety. Do not go out in the dark.

It is much wiser to stay secure during the night-time hours and sleep. It may not be much safer in the light but at least you will be able to see your surroundings, your enemy and all escape routes and will have a better chance of sensible reaction and survival.

FACT 1: If you are in an urban area that still has power and streetlights, it is marginally safer to go out at night. We still recommend saving your scavenging times for the daytime though, as who knows when the power will finally go off.

FACT 2: The closer you are to the North and South poles, the longer the periods of night, and therefore darkness, so you may have to come up with a way of braving the darkness or prepare for a long-haul buckle down in your safe house. For example, Barrow, Alaska has 720 hours of darkness in one period. That's 30 days of night – and in that area you'll also have vampires to worry about. Bummer.

DECAPITATION

The only way to kill a zombie is to *destroy* the brain (see **Brain**) and it is a common misconception that decapitation does just as good a job. Chopping off a zombie's head does stop it from advancing towards you because it has no body – *but it does not kill the zombie*. What you have left is a zombie head that can still infect you – as it can still bite. So although you have technically neutralised the threat, do everyone a favour and finish the job. It will only be a matter of time before you forget you had that head in the corner and you stub your toe on its teeth. Or it could pull itself along by its chin until it manages to reach you while you are sleeping. And if you are lying down with your legs spread, heaven knows where it might choose to bite! Decapitation may seem like fun, but not when you have a severed head attached to your gonads. Destroy the brain.

Also note that it is unwise to collect zombie heads to create your own puppet theatre.

DECISIONS/DELIBERATION

Generally speaking, human beings, particularly the British, don't like to rock the boat and prefer to avoid conflict. That's why it's common to hear 'I'm easy' or 'You decide'.

But I'm here to tell you No! No! And thrice NO! The time for social niceties must cease at the rise of the dead. If you are to survive you must be able to make decisions in a split second and not rely on the opinions or preferences of the rest of your group. Sometimes immediate action is needed in order to stay alive. Imagine a stranger comes to the door of your safe house looking for sanctuary. He is covered in blood. This could be from killing zombies or it could be from wounds…a bite! You could hold a meeting to decide if this stranger is allowed to stay. In the meantime, he has died, risen and infected half of your team including your aged, infertile but quite doting mother who was tending to him and making him a lovely cup of lemon earl grey. Alternatively, you could take it upon yourself to make a quick decision without hours of deliberation and stick a pickaxe in his head. The problem is now gone and you can continue worrying about your own survival rather than random, possibly infected strangers who are liable to sink their teeth into your mother.

Becoming a person who acts in this way can be quite difficult to master so it is wise to start practising now. It doesn't take much and it won't require sticking a pickaxe in someone's head (unless you really want to). All you have to do is start making decisions. So, should your partner ask what you want for dinner, don't say: 'I don't mind, whatever...' Instead reply with a forceful cry of 'PIE! And now!'

Also start making split-second decisions on your own. If you are walking down the street, suddenly decide to cross the road. Don't stop and think, just step out into the oncoming traffic. Make the decision to be on the other side of the road and go for it! If you get hit, you'll heal, and should you die, who has to live with the consequences? Not you!

Obviously your friends and family will start to notice a change in you – a change they may not like. To them you may seem impulsive, selfish and rash. Bear in mind, though, that these people may rely on you when the apocalypse comes and if you don't make the decision to change right now, what's going to happen to your mother when that stranger comes calling? You know I'm right. Sit down and think about it for a while.

DEMOGRAPHICS

Population statistics are scrutinised by marketing companies to find out basic information about their customers (e.g. age, social standing, sex, race, shoe size – generally only shoe marketing companies insist on knowing this last piece of info). You too should be paying attention to these stats as knowledge of basic demographics and common sense can give you incredible foresight in a zombie apocalypse.

Once the apocalypse is in full swing you need to be able

to use good judgement to decide on the best places to attain supplies and set up safe-havens. In order to do this you need to guess which locations nearby are likely to be less infested than others. This is where simple demographic knowledge comes in handy.

If, at the outbreak of the rise of the dead, a Chippendales concert was taking place at a local theatre we could surmise that this specific theatre would be full of female zombies between the ages of 18–50 and a few twenty-something male zombies in various states of undress. It would be unwise to attempt to enter this area as theatres have limited exit points and the Chippendales are relatively popular. This means you will have a building full of zombies, some of whom are younger and therefore stronger.

Using the same process of demographic analysis we can assume that if an old folks home is infested, this will give rise to mostly older zombies who will be easier to defeat due to brittle bones, bad hips or being wheelchair bound (congenital ailments from life pass on to zombies – see: **Physical Ailments**). It will therefore be easier to scavenge there.

This process can be applied to most areas (gyms = young and fit zombies; schools = child zombies; garden centres = families and middle-aged zombies who are stuck in a rut and feel their life has been one long waste).

The only areas we cannot apply this to are panic zones (see **Panic Zones**) – the places most people rush to in times of crisis. These include hospitals, police stations, airports – the areas that we know are the most dangerous. Although there will be a high mix of age, sex and race, we also know that the demographic ratio for panic zones will be 100% dumbass.

DRUGS

The School of Survival does not advocate the use of any recreational drugs, especially when the apocalypse has finally begun. You may think that taking illegal substances to enhance your mood or physical state would be a good idea when battling the undead (and due to the collapse of society and its moral values, previously banned substances will no longer carry a usage penalty), but the cons far outweigh the pros when it comes to drug use. Although you will feel euphoric, strong and possibly fearless for a period of time, after the effects of the drug have worn off you will suffer a longer period of comedown which will leave you more susceptible and less able to cope with attacks.

Addiction is also an issue and the supply of any recreational drugs during the apocalypse will be short at best, so should you become addicted and then be forced into cold turkey your mental process will become erratic, putting yourself and your team in danger.

Not all drugs are bad, though. We wholly endorse the use of steroids during an apocalypse in order to get yourself in peak physical condition as quickly as possible. Although the same rules apply regarding the legality of this issue – do not use prior to the apocalypse, but afterwards anything goes!

There is also the very interesting possibility of using psychotropic drugs as weapons against zombies. Drugs like LSD, Cannabis and Ecstasy are all mind-altering substances which affect the brain. As the brain is the only operating organ in a zombie, would these drugs be useful? Depending on the dosage, it probably wouldn't kill a zombie but it may disorientate them for a while giving you a chance to escape (this could be particularly useful when faced with large crowds of the undead).

The only problem is how to administer the drugs. As the circulatory, respiratory and digestive functions of a zombie are all non-functioning the only possible way to feed the drug into the brain would be to inject it straight into the head. But if you were close enough to stick a syringe into a zombie's cranium, you might as well use a cutlass and get the job done rather than stand there watching a corpse freak out at the sight of its own fingers.

Should you decide to follow experimentation of drugged up zombies further we recommend caution regarding cannabis as we can't be held accountable for what should happen if a member of the undead gets the munchies.

ELECTRICITY

Electricity is an integral part of our daily lives. We use it for watching TV, lighting our homes, running our computers, blowing up bouncy castles with electrically powered pumps, the list is endless. So how will we cope without it? That is something you are going to have to think about long and hard because there will come the time when the lights will go out.

Electricity enables the majority of our leisure-time activities: television, computers and games consoles. Without these items and with loads of time on our hands, we will have to face reality and actually talk to other people. And if there's no alcohol, we'll have to do it whilst sober. Come on, calm down! There are still people alive today who remember a world without all this technology we have now. During the Blitz of the Second World War they used to sit in subways and whisper stories to each other so the aeroplanes didn't hear them. They talked, played games, shared experiences, learnt about each other... Sounds like hell, doesn't it? But it's the only thing you can do unless you've got a generator or solar power unit on your roof...

Actually, that might be better, yes. Go out and buy solar panels and a generator too just in case. That way at least you can watch DVDs or play on your Xbox and not have to suffer another round of Twister with your strange uncle Frank who wears his trousers too high and looks at you funny and just happened to be visiting when news of the apocalypse came through so decided to invite himself to stay with you. If only you could get yourself alone with him for five minutes – just enough time to shove him out of the upstairs window into the arms of the hordes below... Anyway, yes, buy a generator – I've just seen them on eBay for around £150.

ELECTROCONVULSIVE THERAPY

The treatment of certain mental disorders by passing an electrical current directly through the brain. So with that in mind, can you kill a zombie's brain with electricity?

The simple answer is that you can fry just about any organic matter to a crisp if you use enough electricity and a zombie's body will react much in the same way as a human's if it comes into contact with a high enough current (it will conduct the current and so will be held to the spot and shudder). The problem is that the current would have to be quite high as zombies will react to low-voltage shocks in much the same way they react to any pain (i.e. they won't notice it).

So, why would you want to waste your electricity on such a highfalutin, complicated way of killing zombies when you've only got £4.72 on the meter and a pointy stick would do the job just as well? If you have access to the national grid then by all means use this method. Otherwise save your electricity for heating your Super Noodles; they taste horrible cold.

EMOTION

During an apocalypse, one of the major disadvantages we will have as humans (unless you're not human – maybe you're a dolphin and if so kudos to you for taking the next step in your evolution and learning to read) is that we will have to deal with our emotions.

Anger may send you running into a horde of zombies with nothing but a tea strainer to exact revenge for the death of a loved one. Love may stop you from sticking that pitchfork in your wife's head once you've discovered that she's been bitten. Fear may make you wet yourself and the only store where you can get replacement trousers could be infested with zombies meaning you have to survive without pants.

We must learn to control our emotions (I don't mean quash them either as that will just cause ambivalence which is equally as self-destructive; you will hinder your survival if you don't care). You must put that tea strainer to better use and make a nice calming cup of tea and learn to channel your anger into a positive force for destruction so that you can plan well-formulated attacks. Realise that the greatest gift of love you can give your wife is to plunge that garden implement into her head. And you must see that although your fear is not irrational, allowing it to control your bowels is never a positive thing.

Focus on the positive emotions that will help you through these dark days: feel a twinge of anticipation that you are finally able to use your years of training; feel a great sense of responsibility knowing that you can beat this apocalypse; and maybe, just maybe, you'll even feel slightly aroused too (but each to their own).

EMULATION

An interesting school of thought suggests that the best way to survive a zombie apocalypse is to pretend to *be* a zombie and then they won't notice you. Would that work? I don't know. Why don't you wait for the dead to rise and then go and stand in the middle of a horde with your arms outstretched groaning the word 'Braaaaaiiiins!' Go on, give it a shot. I'm sure you'll be fine! Hey, maybe you'll even make some zombie friends and then you can go and have zombie tea parties and shop for new zombie clothes and braid each other's zombie hair whilst giggling over how Zombie Chantelle keeps tripping over her own intestines. Oh! I know! Why don't you sprout wings and go and live on the moon when the apocalypse starts. Someone once said it was made of cheese so you'll have loads to eat! Yeah! What a great idea! *Idiots.*

ENERGY BAR

Looking like blocks of dried-up vomit hardly makes this foodstuff seem appealing, but packed as they are with carbohydrates they are the perfect meal supplement to carry round with you to keep hunger at bay. When scavenging, always fill your trolley with these little beauties and you will never go wrong. Due to their consistency they are also perfect for barricade building and can cause serious damage when thrown with force.

ENERGY DRINK

The most noticeable difference between energy bars and energy drinks is that one is solid whilst the other is liquid. The important thing about this fact is if you needed this explained to you, then prepare to die. You're not going to survive – in fact, I'm surprised you've lasted this long. Maybe it would be best if you didn't leave the house again. Ever.

ENTRAILS

Entrails and intestines are inside of us and the bits that are likely to fall out of us should somebody make a deep enough cut across our midsection. It is worth noting that during a zombie apocalypse you are likely to see your fair share of entrails protruding from zombies and you need to be prepared for this.

You may think that watching a lot of horror films will desensitise you to much of the gore you will encounter on a day to day basis, but we can assure you that this will not be the case. In addition to the sight of dripping entrails, there will also be the overpowering stench and the sound of killing to contend with, and this onslaught cannot be fully appreciated on celluloid.

A simple yet effective way of learning how to cope with entrails is to befriend a local butcher and have them supply you with offal. Once you have acquired this product get your friends or family to strap it to their midriff and keep it there for an indefinite period of time. Watching your mum go about her daily tasks with pig intestines wrapped around her, smelling like an abandoned abattoir will soon have you prepared for facing the real deal.

ESCHEAT

This is a word not commonly used in everyday conversation – 'Excuse me, could you pass the escheat?' or 'What a lovely escheat, where did you get it? It is actually an old common-law doctrine that is very useful to be aware of during a zombie apocalypse.

Along with its partner in doctrine, *bona vacantia*, the basis of these laws is that if a person dies with no will and no heirs then everything they own goes to the crown, the state or immediately superior feudal landlord depending on where you reside.

Land or property ownership may not be exactly high on your agenda when there are crowds of corpses on your tail, but you must never live day to day. You must always plan for the future when mankind inevitably wins the war against the dead.

The important fact to note about this law is that the property of the deceased is claimed by the crown or the government.

When the apocalypse begins one of two things will have happened to these two institutions. They will:

1) Have been ushered into steel-walled underground bunkers by men in dark suits and sunglasses shouting 'Down! Down!' and 'The eagle is in the nest!' where they will have innumerable supplies to see out these dark days, or

2) Be dead.

In either scenario they'll be out of the way leaving you to declare yourself the new superior feudal lord of any particular area of the country. This then gives you the right to claim all the property of everyone who has died with no living heirs (of which I would imagine there would be a fair few). Of course, there will be those people who will merely think you have gone insane and disregard this law and your claims. They will argue that as there is no government to uphold the law that the law is null and void. If this is the case then feel free to declare yourself Prime Minister or even Queen which gives you the right to make up whatever laws you want and uphold them as best you can.

There are, of course, easier ways of obtaining property in a lawless society which usually involves a large angry posse and a stash of weapons. But even if you do decide to go down that path, at least you know now that the law is on your side.

ESPRESSO

Caffeine taken in excess is thought to induce blurred vision, dizziness, insomnia, anxiety and fruity breath to name but a few of the symptoms. However, I simply cannot envisage waking up in the morning with a mob of undead to dispose of without a double espresso to get the motor running. Seeing as I will have to forego most other pleasures in life whilst my dead relatives plunder the earth I am not giving up coffee. And whilst I understand that eventually my supplies will run out, woe betide the person who has to face me in the morning to explain that there are no more beans – and heaven help them if they offer me tea instead!

At least there'll be a lot of zombies annihilated that day. Which is never a bad thing…

That doesn't mean that anyone surviving alongside me should pretend there's no coffee just to get me angry – just the thought upsets me!

I need a coffee – now!

EUTHANASIA

Assisted suicide is a sticky subject at the best of times. It is, of course, currently illegal in the eyes of the law but there are people who are compelled to ignore the law in order to alleviate the suffering of their loved ones. In the case of a zombie apocalypse, whatever your feelings on the subject, euthanasia will become common practice.

It is common knowledge that when bitten it is only a matter of time before a person becomes a zombie and the only way to stop this *before* it happens is to kill them by destroying the brain. If guns are in short supply it will be very difficult to commit suicide and destroy the brain at the same time so it is likely that you will be asked to help. Do not shun your responsibility. Better to do it now than when they are trying to bite you.

It is also worth noting that even if guns are available, some religions and cultures see suicide as a sin that will condemn them to hell. They will not in all good conscience be able to kill themselves even though they are aware of the alternative. Again, you must step up to the plate and do the deed. Bear in mind that the act of taking another human's life must not be taken lightly whatever the circumstances. There may be people in your group who hinder you, are too slow, complain too much or you just don't like. You cannot just kill them for no good reason – at least wait until they tell you they have a headache or an ingrown toe-nail. The main aim of euthanasia is to alleviate suffering and you'll be doing them a favour.

EXPLOSIVES

Although it may seem like a fun idea to throw highly charged incendiary devices at the living dead, it is not always the most effective way to dispose of them. Remember that the only way to kill a zombie is to destroy its brain. Blowing it up does not always guarantee this. When you throw an explosive device the chances are that it will land on the floor before it explodes. Likewise, if you plant mines or booby traps they are also going to be triggered at ground level. Depending on the level of the explosive this will at least blow the zombies legs off, but that's not going to stop the blighters, is it and they'll just keep coming, dragging themselves across the floor towards you? Even if you manage to do serious damage to the walking corpses and blow their bodies apart you could still be left with a worst-case scenario of a head being blown off right into your lap without the brain being destroyed and the mouth fully operational!

Using explosives will also cause smoke, flames and debris – all things that will affect your fighting environment and your vision but not the zombies', putting you at an immediate disadvantage.

Even utilising explosives to take out whole buildings full of infected bodies is not an incredibly smart idea. Again, there is no guarantee that the dead within your target building will be killed and they could just be buried and either burrow out over time or be dug up by other survivors when the area is assumed safe.

If explosives should be used for anything it is for creating fortification. They can be used to quickly block roads and tunnels and take out bridges meaning you can make areas safer for yourself as you cut off access points for the undead.

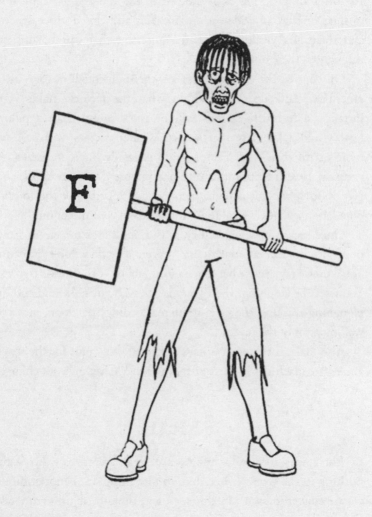

FACTORY

Factories are great places to hide when the apocalypse begins due to their mixture of wide open-plan areas and closed office spaces, and there is a wealth of useful equipment that can be utilised throughout these buildings.

Of course, the effectiveness of the individual factory as a sanctuary really does depend on what the factory makes. For instance, a furniture factory will be more useful than a pillow factory and a Japanese martial arts weapon factory will be even more useful than that. Factories are generally built on estates so you may have the option to pick and choose if you are quick and give yourself enough time to secure the factory before the zombie population reaches critical mass and heads in your direction.

Once secure in your factory, it is a good idea to refrain from operating unfamiliar machinery – even if it does look like fun. You know very well what I'm talking about – the forklift truck. You won't be laughing when you hit reverse by mistake and end up ploughing through the steel-shuttered loading bay doors into the waiting arms of the undead.

Also make sure that you have a pocketful of coins for the snack and coffee machines in the staffroom as they never give out change.

FERAL

By their very nature zombies are feral creatures who want nothing in the world other than to bite things. It is not zombies we are concerned with in this segment, though, as unfortunately they will not be our only threat during the apocalypse. Other feral creatures can also cause us problems. Let's take a look at them.

Wild animals - feral

Rats, badgers and mountain lions will all become more widespread when they realise civilisation has ceased. They will be more prevalent in urban areas and less afraid of humans.

Domestic animals - feral

Left to fend for themselves they will revert to the ways of the wild to survive. Danger level depends on the animal. Dogs will be more dangerous than budgies.

Children - feral

Depending on the time they have been alone they will become more and more animal-like – much like Tarzan or Mowgli. Highly unlikely to attack. Hiding and stealth will be their modus operandi, and stealing supplies will be the main issue you have with them.

Adults - feral

The most dangerous of the lot – as becoming feral will have more to do with mental issues than necessity for survival like the other examples. They will attack you, they will try to kill you and they will smell.

Colin - feral

I think this one's a typo but I believe he can be a bit of a rough diamond. You certainly wouldn't want to rub him up the wrong way. Not sure if he'd attack you – maybe if you were taking pictures?

FIGHTING STYLE

There are many different fighting styles that can be adopted when attempting to fend off a member of the undead. Realistically, when it comes down to the nitty-gritty, many of these styles will be replaced by you manically swiping at your attacker with a blunt instrument whilst screaming insanely.

It is worth noting, though, for those of you who do manage to keep your cool during a zombie apocalypse, that the majority of fighting styles don't take into account a zombie's primary weapon: its mouth.

A zombie will attack with its mouth and grab with its hands. It will not punch, kick, roundhouse, forward roll, fly like a butterfly or sting like a frog. Its primary goal is to get a part of your body into its mouth and that is where some fighting styles will fall short – mainly because biting and grabbing are seen as illegal moves and a little bit girly. Hence, if you were ring-fighting professionally, the bout would have been halted and the person biting would have had a finger wagged at them (we all know that if you wagged a finger at a zombie you would get it bitten off so don't be thinking of trying that).

What is also frowned upon in many fighting styles is multiple head shots. This can lead to brain damage of your opponent – which when fighting a zombie is pretty much the point. With this in mind you need to be able to adapt your fighting styles to be most effective.

FIGHTING RULES

1) Avoid being bitten.

2) Avoid being grabbed – and if you are grabbed, escape whilst following point one and attempting point three.

3) Destroy the brain whilst carrying out both points one and two.

4) Doing point one, point two and point three all at the same time can effectively be called point four.

5) There is no point five unless you want to incorporate point four into the other three points thus making the need for a further point, but if that were the case we could just continue to bullet point the points we had already made in order to make pointless points so disregard this point.

FIGHTING TALK

No matter what your fighting style, it is always good to use as much profanity as possible. It's the done thing. You should swear and insult with such vehemence that you spit whilst you are doing it. Do not worry about the noise you are making either. Once a zombie has you and starts growling others will be attracted anyway and a good bit of swearing can pump you up enough to finish the zombie off quicker and escape before his friends arrive. PLEASE note that words like 'poo', 'bottom', 'nipple' and 'flip' do not class as swearing.

All other moves you incorporate into your own personal fighting style will be purely for show – and frankly a zombie isn't going to be impressed if you can kick a lighted cigarette from his mouth whilst standing on a bottle of beer, so what's the use of adding razzle-dazzle if it's only going to be as effective as flailing about with a hammer and swearing very loudly?

FILM

Many people would not appreciate the merits of sitting in a darkened room surrounded by empty Wotsit packets, pizza boxes and coffee cups watching horror films. They would prefer to go for a jog around the block in order to be in peak physical condition in preparation for the apocalypse. Whilst I fully support exercise as essential to a decent training regime, so is research and the only way we can research zombies is by watching films.

A zombie apocalypse has not yet happened so our only source of reference is the imagination of such masters as Romero and Pegg. Although some of the technicalities may not be correct (*Day of the Dead 2008*, for example – I don't think we'll ever see vegetarian zombies or watch them disintegrate when touched by flame) they provide us with some noteworthy combat and survival ideas. Who previously would have thought of using LPs as weapons prior to *Shaun of the Dead*? The issue of zombies underwater had never really been broached prior to *Land of the Dead* and to give *Day of the Dead 2008* some credit, zombies may well inadvertently let off a machine gun. Who knows? And that is the point – nobody *does* know and we won't until it finally happens, but we need to attain as much information as possible for every available scenario if we are going to be prepared. So yes, go for a jog around the block, but also watch zombie films. Lots of them! (We also recommend interspersing the horrors with the occasional romantic comedy just to take the edge off. And maybe some porn? But not if you're eating Wotsits as that will turn your penis orange.)

FIRE

Without electricity, fire may be our only option for light or cooking. In these circumstances, when used properly so that the flames or smoke will not attract hordes to your location, we advocate its use. Never, never, NEVER use fire as a weapon.

We know that the only way to kill a zombie is by destroying the brain and I'm only repeating myself now in case certain readers decided to skip the letters A–E due to some particular dislike of those specific letters and have joined us straight at F.

Fire will destroy a brain, and indeed an entire human body given time, but when you have a member of Club Dead shambling towards you, time is something that is not on your side. Zombies are unaffected by pain and have no fear, so being set alight will do nothing to deter them from continuing on their quest to bite you. So now, because you threw a Molotov at your attacker, you not only have a zombie shambling towards you but you have a flaming zombie who has just set fire to your mum's favourite curtains and isn't stopping.

The fact that the zombie is a walking fireball will prevent you from getting close enough with a melee weapon (see **Weapons**) and to make matters worse, your mother will be shouting about her curtains and the ash that's being shed on her Laura Ashley sofa. So, you see what you've done? Not only have you condemned yourself to death, you've also burnt down your own safe house. Rather than make a Molotov cocktail, you should have just smashed the bottle over the zombie's head and then rammed the jagged edge into its frontal lobe. OK, you would have got blood on the carpet, but I'm reliably informed that club soda could get that out.

FIRST AID

There will be times during an apocalypse when non-zombie-related accidents happen and you won't have the excuse of just being able to smash the injured party in the head with a brick in order to solve the problem. A good survivalist needs to know the basics of first aid in order to keep the rest of the team in tip-top condition ready for their next round with the undead.

First aid and medical issues are quite involved and you could probably fill a whole book with the various skills you'd need to learn to deal with the injuries that could befall you or a member of your team during a zombie apocalypse (in fact, I did fill a book with the info called *Dr Dale's Various Skills You'd Need to Learn to Deal With the Injuries that Could Befall You or a Member of Your Team During a Zombie Apocalypse* – available from all good bookshops soon). In the meantime though, I have listed some of the more pertinent information should the dead rise before the book is released.

Dislocated bones

We've all seen it happen in films where someone has to have their shoulder popped back in by a buddy. Well, if you've seen it in a film you shouldn't need me to tell you about it. Thing is, it's not really as easy as it looks and it may take three or four (or fifteen is my personal best) attempts to get that bone back in place. Naturally, the person with the injury will feel one or two slight twinges of pain so you may have to ram a balled-up sock in their mouth to muffle any screams. Do ensure that you don't push the sock too far into their mouth as this will suffocate them.

Suffocation with sock

The quickest and easiest way to deal with this is to remove the sock. However, should the sock have been shoved too far down the throat for you to able to retrieve it then you may have to perform a tracheotomy. This would involve making a hole in the person's throat in order for them to continue to breath. It's usually best not to do this unless you are a trained surgeon, but if you don't happen to be qualified then please be careful not to damage the vocal chords when carrying out the procedure. If you do, it means that the injured person may no longer be able to speak or will sound like a Dalek when they do.

If the person is still conscious when you carry out the procedure, make sure someone holds them down as, should they struggle, it may cause you to slip whilst making the incision and cut open your own hand.

Cut on hand caused by accident during tracheotomy

As long as you don't slice any major arteries there should be no problems. The initial order of the day is to stop the bleeding. Just apply pressure to the wound until the blood starts to congeal. If it is a small wound this can be done with a small piece of tissue and your finger. If the wound is larger use a towel and your entire hand. Also make sure your hand is elevated to slow the flow of blood to the wound, giving the cut time to start healing.

Once the blood has subsided, ensure the wound is clean and bandaged. Do ensure that the bandages are tied tightly though, so they do not come loose and you inadvertently trip over them and break your arm.

Broken arm after inadvertently tripping over loose bandages

If after the fall the arm is twisted into a strange shape, you may wish to take a moment to assess the situation. You will then realise that as you are in the middle of an apocalypse there is no medical help coming, and you will come to the conclusion that you didn't actually need to assess the situation. The arm will need to be splinted so that it resets in an approximation of the shape it first started out in. To do this, you will need to twist the arm round, back into its original position and then bind a splint to it (a splint is a solid unbendable piece of wood. If the splint has nails sticking out of it or a spike on the end, and is bound to the broken arm effectively, it can also be used as a weapon).

Be aware that if you have to twist the broken arm back into its original position, the injured party may struggle with pain and inadvertently push you through a plate glass window.

Being pushed through a plate glass window by a struggling person with a broken arm

As long as no shards of glass have pierced vital organs or major arteries you should be OK. Just slowly remove the slivers of glass that are protruding from your body and apply pressure to the wounds much like you would if you had cut your hand whilst performing a tracheotomy. If there are larger pieces of glass it may be wise to have a sewing kit at hand so that the wound can be stitched up to aid the healing process. The sewing kit need not have any more in it than a needle and thread because if it is too heavy somebody may dislocate their shoulder when lifting it.

Dislocated shoulder from lifting a heavy sewing box

Refer back to the beginning.

These are just a few of the possible accidents that could occur whilst trying to survive the zombie apocalypse. It is best to assess each case individually and decide whether or not you are going to spend the time and energy treating the injured party.

For example: How long will your teammate be out of service with the injury? Will your teammate suffer long-term effects due to the injury? Will they get a lot of sympathy and attention from the rest of the team leaving you wanting? Once you've weighed up the pros and cons you should be able to decide whether you will help your injured teammate or whether you should creep up to them in the night, stick a bag on their head and dump them in the middle of the city to wait to die. I'm sure they'd want the latter – no one wants to be a burden in this day and age.

FOOTWEAR

We have previously discussed the best clothing to wear during an apocalypse and equally important is planning what to wear on your feet. Your feet, along with your legs, are what you will do most of your running with so it is important that they are correctly attired. We recommend steel toe-capped workmen's boots or any variation thereof. Initially, they may seem cumbersome to run any great distance in, but with the potential for hazards and rough terrain they are preferable to normal running shoes and the toe-caps give an added kick when your feet are needed to stave off attackers.

FOOTWEAR AT HOME

Of course, this is what we recommend when out and about on the scavenge or on the move. When in the confines of your safe house you can afford to be a little more comfort-orientated or adventurous with your footwear (I do enjoy a lovely red stiletto with a killer heel) as long as you have your boots ready should you need to leave quickly.

FRIENDS AND FAMILY

You will no doubt be familiar with the saying 'Keep your friends close, but your enemies closer'. This doesn't apply in a zombie apocalypse. Bugger your enemies (not literally) and, if possible, use them as a decoy to facilitate your own escape. It is your friends and family who are most important to you now.

First of all we're going to do a little exercise. I want you to close your eyes and picture all of your family together – perhaps envision them posing for a family portrait that you are taking. Now I want you to imagine which two of your family you would take with you if there was a zombie apocalypse. It doesn't matter what your reasons are – just pick two. Next... Oh, actually, there is no next and you can open your eyes now. (Don't think

I didn't know you hadn't actually closed your eyes in the first place – if you had closed your eyes you wouldn't have been able to read where I told you to open them again! Next time do as you're told!)

What you did just then was decide who to save. It will be impossible to save everyone so what you have to do is *prioritise*. Of course, you may manage more than two. If your entire family lives under one roof then you'll have a good chance of saving them all (but remember, the benefit system will crumble during an apocalypse so you may have to find some other way to survive). It is important to realise, though, that if your family is separated some of them will die. It also doesn't matter what your reasons for choosing your top two were. OK, granted your sister is younger than your grandma – but granny was the only one who was ever nice to you and your sister always thought she was better than you what with getting her degree in natural sciences and marrying that marine biologist – you'll show her who the golden girl of the family is now! You must help the ones you feel are most important to you as their support will guide you through the darker days of the siege.

Your friends are just as important, but bear in mind that each individual friend will have family members that they will wish to save in an apocalypse so it is with your friends that you need to make a survival plan. Firstly, decide where you plan to meet within seven days of the outbreak. I will leave you to decide on an exact location – there is enough information within this dictionary to help you make an informed decision.

But before we leave this topic let's do another quick exercise. I want you to put your friends in order of usefulness during a zombie apocalypse. For example, a martial arts expert would be very useful whereas a performing arts student would not.

Once you have done that, look at the list and ask yourself the question: 'Are there enough skilled people in my circle of friends?' If not, then you need to make some new friends. Mechanics, nurses, weapons forgers – get on MySpace, Facebook and sadandlonely.com and link up with people of use in your area.

'You can choose your friends but you can't choose your family.' Remember that! It will come in handy. Although technically it is now no longer true. You can legally divorce your own parents and get a Professor of Medicine or Chuck Norris to adopt you – then they'd be duty bound to protect you when the zombies rise.

FUNFAIR

There may be numerous places to hide in a funfair – like the hall of mirrors and the fun house – and there'll be rides and rollercoasters and an endless supply of candyfloss, so initially it may seem like the perfect place to set up your sanctuary. But if *Zombieland* has taught us anything it's that when the apocalypse comes there will be zombie clowns, and where will they be? The funfair, of course.

Clowns are bad enough when they're not the reanimated dead but when they are they're twice as freaky. Besides, it would be extremely embarrassing if you were attacked and then had to explain to everyone that you were bitten by a clown. Especially if it was a girl clown with big shoes and a pink wig and a nose that honked when you hit her.

Mascots are an issue too – people dressed as animals. It's demeaning enough that they had to do the job when they were alive, but now they have to spend eternity wandering round looking like that, and would you really feel right taking a machete to a six foot zombie beaver called Bradley? Or a puffin called Don?

GAMING

Specifically, gaming that involves a console and not gaming that requires you to sit at a dining room table wearing a plastic replica helmet pretending that you're Bladmor the invisible wizard from the realm of Juggerjuggerjuggersadlife.

Unlike most survival manifestos for the coming apocalypse, we fully advocate the use of video gaming as part of your training routine. It has been shown that along with regular exercise and occasional forays into fresh air, console gaming can increase hand-eye coordination, reaction time and stamina. Just ensure that you train by playing relevant games and do not lose your focus on facts and reality. It may be a great deal of fun to pretend to be a small fat Italian plumber racing a dragon in a go-cart, but at exactly what point during a zombie apocalypse do you think you will have to utilise that particular skill? And even if you do think you look particularly snazzy in a pair of red cut-off dungarees, I can assure you that no matter how many mushrooms you eat you will neither become invincible for a short period of time nor will any part of your body increase in size.

Even in zombie-specific games, there are certain occurrences that must be taken with a pinch of salt. Firstly, you are not going to find small caches of ammo and guns piled up in safe rooms for you to stock up on, and if you do have weapons they will take longer to load than the click of a button. Neither will you be able to heal yourself with a few sprigs of basil and a lettuce leaf or by wrapping a bandage around your leg for five seconds.

GARAGE

I've just been down to my garage and found a life-sized plastic carp and a copy of the 1984 winners of the Eurovision Song Contest on vinyl 45. It is amazing what you can find in these oft-ignored store areas when preparing for and scavenging during a zombie apocalypse. The average household tends to store all their tools in the garage, along with batteries, fuel, light bulbs, rope, old clothes, hiking boots, winter coats and freezers full of food – some people even keep their cars in there! Garages are also safer areas to scavenge in than houses as you are more likely to encounter the zombified inhabitants still in situ in their living room where they thought they were safe. People often opt for comfort over security in these situations and nine out of ten homeowners would prefer to die in their own houses than in their garage (the other one out of ten actually lived in his garage so the results there are a bit cloudy).

Although I have been extolling the virtue of the humble

garage I would not go so far as recommending it as a safe house. Although they are generally secure, should the main entrance become compromised it is a very large opening for a lot of zombies to pour through at the same time, leaving you little time for response or manoeuvre. Also, they are on the ground floor and as we all know the higher up you go, the safer you are. No, just leave garages for your shopping trips – you'll be surprised at what you find.

> **TURNING GARAGE JUNK INTO ZOMBIE WEAPONS**
>
> I would use my carp as a stabbing weapon after first sharpening the nose to a deadly point. The record I would use to lift the spirits of my comrades in times of hardship. There is nothing like the uplifting Swedish melody of 'Diggi-Loo Diggi-Ley'. And if we didn't have a record player we'd just look at the sleeve photo – the Herrys could cheer anyone up.

GARDEN CENTRE

The perfect place to find weapons during a zombie apocalypse. Who needs guns when in these veritable goldmines you can pick up shears, strimmers, axes, chainsaws, pitchforks, scythes, and electric lawnmowers? Those who like to be inventive in their zombie-killing methods could spend hours filling up their vans with all manner of damage-dealing tools.

For the non-lethal minded there is also the option of stocking up on seeds and plants with which to grow your own foodstuffs to aid your survival. Of course, these should be saved for when you have found a secure location for a long-term stay (but if the worst comes to the worst you could always just eat the seeds – I am assured that plants will not grow in your stomach as a school friend informed me they would when I swallowed an apple pip as a child – the fact I don't have an apple tree sprouting from my head should be proof enough for that).

Be warned though, a garden centre will not be a safe haven in the apocalypse. Firstly, there will be other people who will have thought of the possibility of finding weapons and food there, which means you may have a fight on your hands to get the best hardware – who'd want to take out a member of the undead with the 300mm Sarel Spiker lawn aerator when you have the option of using the 900mm?

As well as the living there is a high possibility that you will have to face the dead too. These days garden centres boast coffee shops, gift shops and all manner of other non-garden-related paraphernalia so people tend to spend whole days in these places. There is one consolation to this – but refer to the entry under **Demographics** for more information.

Finally, do not think of using a garden centre as your base of operations. The buildings are primarily made of glass. See the problem there? Yes, it will be a nightmare to keep clean.

GARLIC

Garlic cannot be used to ward off the undead unless the undead you happen to be warding off are vampires (which is a completely new book waiting to happen) so do not wander around an apocalyptic Earth with a clove of garlic around your neck – people will just think you're silly.

GIRAFFE

The GIRAFFE AMB Radar defence and surveillance system used by the military provides 3D target updates over a large elevation range at a rate of one-per-second. Ultra-low antenna side-lobes combined with pulse-to-pulse and burst-to-burst frequency agility provides some resistance to jamming. Those of you who own one of these will be fully aware of its operation and capabilities and those that don't own one probably never will which is why we won't be talking about it today. Instead we'll be discussing the giraffe, the tallest of all land-living animal species and the perfect mode of transport during a zombie apocalypse.

Giraffes are currently on the 'low concern' list by the International Union for Conservation of Nature, which obviously means that they are easy to come by. So if you're able to nab yourself a giraffe, get one whilst they're hot.

The average speed of a giraffe can be up to 55 mph and their height (up to 18 ft) means that you can travel on the back of one through a horde of zombies without having to worry about being grabbed. Although you may have some concerns over the well-being of your steed, remember that giraffes are more than capable of looking after themselves. One kick from an adult giraffe is capable of smashing in a lion's skull or snapping its spine. Using a giraffe as a ladder as well as a mode of transport will allow you to reach windows on the first and second floors of buildings without having to enter at the ground floor, making scavenging missions easier.

The only minor problem we can see in keeping a giraffe during a zombie apocalypse is that you will need a safe house with a very high roof and big door – unless you set up your base in a giraffe enclosure, which will then give you even more giraffes to travel around on and access to other animals at the zoo too (you could train a moose to dance for your enjoyment and penguins to go on kamikaze missions – the possibilities are endless).

GOLF CLUBS

A golf club is a golf club. You just pick it up and smash it into a zombie's skull. Yes? No! Of course, any golf club can be used to dispose of an undead pest, but if you're going to do a job you might as well do it properly and use the best tool for the job.

Golf clubs fall into four main categories: woods, irons, hybrids and putters. Each of these categories is used for a different purpose.

For the sake of simplicity (and so as not to get angry letters from golfing experts) here is a golfing club breakdown:

The **wood** is for long distance shots, the **iron** is for more difficult shots approaching the green (i.e. over the rough, through trees etc.), **hybrids** encompass the virtues of both woods and irons, and **putters** are used for shorter flat shots that require good aim.

As putters are used for short-distance ball-hitting they are not built to withstand heavy usage so we must immediately relegate them to the bottom of our list.

When it comes to woods, it will make a difference depending on if you are using an older or newer set of clubs. Older woods are made from wood, whereas newer woods are made of more durable metals. If it is a wood wood then discard it. Metal is always better.

The most durable club is an iron. They are built for working in the rough so have to withstand the possibility of smacking a tree stump or badger, but don't necessarily have the weight behind them to allow for longer distance hitting.

This leaves us with the hybrid, which with the distance power of a wood and the familiar swing of an iron makes it a perfect brain-smushing weapon.

For those unfamiliar with the world of golfing we would suggest finding out what a hybrid looks like now as you don't want to be wasting time during an attack scrabbling through a golf bag searching for the correct club whilst a zombie is bearing down on you. Just ensure that if you are not a regular golf player you choose a club with an A-Flex shaft to maximise your swing. Of course, the pros amongst you should always stick with an X-Flex; you know what I'm talking about… I'm glad somebody does.

GRAFFITI

When the power goes out and you are no longer able to make pretty posters on Microsoft Publisher with smiley-faced clipart you will have to find an alternative way of leaving messages for other survivors other than pinning a note to the door. The most obvious and cleverest way to do this is by using graffiti. This method was used during the Great Plague in London in 1665 when large crosses were drawn on the doors of houses that were infected. Using a similar system in a zombie plague would be useful for various reasons.

Firstly, you would be able to alert fellow survivors that a particular building is highly infested by the undead. By marking buildings with a big red cross, other survivors will know to stay clear of that particular domicile. Of course, this does somewhat negate the selfish attitude you should be adopting, but I suppose there should be some give and take.

Secondly, you could mark a building to let fellow survivors know that it has been drained of all resources. Maybe by writing EMPTY on the door or LOOTED. This is by no means a way to gloat to other survivors that you've got all the Curly Wurlys, but it will save them wasting their time and energy in searching a building that is already empty.

Thirdly, you would be able to let the authorities or other survivors know if you are currently occupying a building. You could daub SAFEHOUSE or SURVIVORS INSIDE on the walls or roof.

There is a condition to sending out this message, though – and that is you should update it daily with the date. Writing SURVIVORS INSIDE is very similar to the notes you see on shop doors that state BACK IN FIVE MINUTES – nobody knows when the five minutes began. If you've just turned up at the shop, they could have already been away four minutes which means you only have a minute to wait. But if they've just closed the door, you may have to hang around for the full five minutes! What do you do? It's so ambiguous! As is the sign SURVIVORS INSIDE. At the onset of the outbreak there could very well have been survivors inside but they may all have moved on now – or worse, they could all be dead which means the sign should read ZOMBIES INSIDE. It is unlikely that anyone will come to your aid unless they are 100% certain that you are still inside and simply updating the sign daily will help.

Another good indicator that there are survivors inside a building will be the masses of zombies outside clamouring to get in. If this is the case, don't bother nipping out to change the sign on the door. Just update the one on the roof and hope that help flies overhead – or an extremely tall soldier walks past.

GUNS

As stated in the introduction, we won't focus heavily on the use of guns as a weapon, but I have two very valid points to make regarding any form of handheld firearm. Firstly, *zombies* with guns. It is highly unlikely that you will come across this scenario, but if you do, you need to be prepared. Zombies will have no comprehension or memory of how to use normal, everyday items like door handles or ladders. The undead are often depicted holding on to everyday items. This is perhaps because they were killed whilst holding them, or because rigor mortis has set in and they are incapable of letting go.

What if a soldier was killed whilst holding his gun? He would reanimate still holding the weapon and although he would have no idea what it was, it could still accidentally go off if he made a sudden movement. How do you combat this problem?

In the same way you would combat a zombie without a gun – just with extra caution. The zombie will be unaware that it can use the weapon to gain an advantage. You, therefore, need to get the headshot in as quickly as possible – you will then have a dead zombie and also a gun to add to your weapons inventory.

The second point I want to make regards gun safety and handling. Remember that guns don't kill people, people kill people – although guns make people's jobs a lot easier when they want to kill other people – but on the other hand people who need people are the luckiest people in the world, whereas people who need guns may still be lucky – just lucky people without guns – and as long as they have people they can still be classed as being lucky, the luckiest people in the world, in fact. I think this is important to remember when handling firearms.

HAIKU

In the apocalypse, culture and the continuance thereof may take a sideline to more important things (e.g. killing the undead, surviving the horror and rebuilding the human race). But we must not lose our history and heritage of creativity because this is what differentiates us from animals (as well as coherent speech, war, religion, the ability to write and opposable thumbs).

Creating art, however, can be a somewhat time-consuming and cumbersome activity, and we won't all have time to sit and create a sprawling oil-painted masterpiece of the City of Naples at Night or devise a new musical based on the life and times of Barbra Streisand.

This is where the Haiku comes in. Short, snappy and to the point, they have all the beauty and meaning of any poem I've ever read but with the bite-sized readability of only being seventeen syllables long.

Learning the art of the Haiku also means that we will be able to entertain each other without the worry of being interrupted by the marauding undead and leaving a performance unfinished.

Take for example one of the most well-known Haiku, Basho's *Old Pond* which goes like this:

> *Furu ike ya*
> *kawazu tobikomu*
> *mizu no oto*

I'll leave you for a moment to soak up the beauty and meaning behind these words – but now let's run this again in a simulation situation.

You: *Furu ike ya kawazu tobikomu* (CRASH! BANG!) Oh no, zombies are getting in!!

Audience: But wait – we haven't heard the end of your poem! This is highly disappointing and unfulfilling.

You: *Mizu no oto.*

Audience: (taking a moment to soak up the beauty and meaning behind the words) Beautiful.

You: Now run!!!

As you can see from that simulation, the audience were not left wondering how your creative masterpiece concluded and also had time to escape. Imagine if you'd had to finish Homer's *Iliad* with over 15,600 verses. I think we can pretty much guarantee you'd all be dead – either from the zombies or from boredom. So, to continue the art of culture and poetry into the post-apocalyptic land, the Haiku is the way forward (and limericks too).

THE ENGLISH TRANSLATION... of Basho's *Old Pond*:

Old Pond…

A frog leaps in

Water's sound.

It does rather lose a lot of its majesty in translation…

HALLOWEEN

There is never really a perfect time for a zombie apocalypse to begin. In fact, any day that portends the beginning of the rise of the dead is going to be a bit crap. And although Halloween is a pagan festival which some see as a celebration of the occult, the apocalypse is no more likely to occur on this day of the year than any other. The problem is that this particular occasion makes a zombie outbreak incredibly difficult to contain as I will explain.

In Western culture, Halloween is 'celebrated' on the 31st October and should that date fall on a weekend the festivities will often extend over several days. That's several days of folks dressing up as ghouls, purposefully making themselves appear dead and spraying fake blood all over the place. With Halloween celebrations increasing in popularity, costumes and spooky effects have become incredibly sophisticated and realistic. This means that it will be more difficult to tell the real zombies from the fake ones. As a result people will become infected very quickly before the authorities or those 'in the know' can leap into action and commence their survival and control plans.

Even once the authorities have become aware of the situation, they will find it difficult to know who to target. The living will be dressed as the dead so the undead will look like the living. But this will in no way stop the living being attacked by the undead (see **Emulation**) and when given no choice the authorities are liable to shoot the living believing them to be the undead, in order to keep themselves from being killed.

Of course, there is nothing we can do to halt the popularity of this festival but what we can do, is ensure that we are kept safe. You must stay vigilant and you must *never* dress as anything that looks vaguely dead. We suggest SpongeBob Squarepants. Even under extreme pressure no member of the authorities would shoot him.

HEAD

The head is the thing on the top of your neck where the brain is stored. In the case of a zombie apocalypse the phrase 'Always go for the brain' can reasonably translate to 'Always go for the head'... What am I telling you this for? You know this, right? Right? Dear god, please tell me you know this! If you didn't know this then when the apocalypse comes, that thing on the top of your neck – yup – that thing with the face on it! Stick it in an oven and turn the gas on... What's an oven? Oh Jeez!

HEDGEHOG

The humble hedgehog comes in for a lot of stick. He is forever being squished on country lanes or being burnt to death when he decides to make his home in our bonfires. So, in order to protect our prickly chum from any further mistreatment, let me just make it very clear from the start that you *cannot use a hedgehog as a weapon*.

Yes, hedgehogs have spines, but contrary to popular belief a hedgehog's spines are liable to do very little damage to a member of the undead. Their spikes have been compared to hairbrush bristles and if one comes into contact with them, the pain level is only as bad as being poked with a pen. This is because a hedgehog's spines are hollow hair made hard by keratin. So, if you had considered taping a hedgehog to a stick and using it as a mace to destroy a zombie's brain, let me assure you, you would have just as much luck if you used a gerbil. So please do not use hedgehogs as weapons. Tortoises on the other hand... Strap them to a stick and their shells can cause major carnage.

HELICOPTER

Do you know how to fly a helicopter? No! Then what is the use of me explaining to you how to use one during a zombie apocalypse? It's not like a bicycle where you can just get on and start peddling. You actually need to know how to use one! There are all kinds of buttons and dials about speed and turbine speed, turbine outlet temperature, horizontal situation indicators, not to mention the ADF and the VOR. Did you really think you could just hop in, turn a key and you'd be off? If you know nothing about helicopters, then forget about them – get a hang glider, or take a course now before the apocalypse begins. Just skip this next bit for now.

If you do know how to fly a helicopter you'd use it to ESCAPE! It's not rocket science! What else are you going to use one for? As a weapon to slice up zombies with the blades in mid-flight? That's just stupid talk!

HELL

When there is no more room in hell, the dead will walk the earth. It's therefore safe to assume that hell won't top the list of best places to be when the apocalypse begins. And the fact that it's so overcrowded will probably make the dead down there even more vicious and angry than the ones who are wandering around on earth. They'll probably keep jostling each other when they're trying to have a sip of their coffee meaning that they'll have Nescafé all down their shirts and there's nothing more frustrating than that. And what makes it worse is there's nowhere in hell to get new clothes (although I believe there are plans to build a Primark down there).

On the other hand, if the dead are shuffling round in hell and on earth, this should mean that heaven is probably quite safe. Although I think the requirements for getting into heaven are quite strict. You've got to have two references and a utility bill at least.

To be honest, you're probably best staying away from most theological locations – stick to finding a nice bunker or revolving sky restaurant to bed down in. Besides, you don't want to have to go to all the trouble of getting into heaven only to have your eyes burnt out and your brain melted purely for looking upon God. Mind you, before that happens you could always ask him why the bloody hell he's let the undead invade earth. And why he keeps letting Noel Edmunds back onto the telly.

HELMET

A cardinal sin in the war against the undead is to wear a helmet. NEVER wear a helmet! Ever! Ever! Ever! Do you hear me? You don't need an explanation – you should have realised by now that I know what I'm talking about! Just don't do it! OK? Never!

HELMET (THE EXPLANATION)

OK, maybe you do need an explanation. A helmet essentially covers the head. That's its job, to protect your noggin (some of you may already have picked up on the reasoning behind the 'no helmet rule' – clever people). So, what happens if you get bitten and turn into a zombie? Your head is protected! How do you kill a zombie? Go for the brain! Thus, you have made the job of other survivors twice as hard because your brain is protected by a helmet!

Of course, you may argue that if you were bitten you would have had the foresight to remove your helmet before you reanimated. And my argument would be, if you were bitten, why wear a helmet in the first place? Because it obviously didn't do its job as you had to remove it because you were bitten!

If any more reason not to wear a helmet were needed, consider that not only will they interfere with peripheral vision but also that most of them cover your ears meaning they will affect your hearing. Now, as I said before – no helmets! So let's just leave it at that and move on.

HIDE/HIDING

The most effective way to survive in a zombie apocalypse. Some believe that going all gung-ho and running about with sharpened weapons hacking up your opponents is the way to survive – but I contest that with the theory that the less time you spend surrounded by the undead, the less chance you will have of being killed. Thus, you survive.

Naturally, there will be times when fighting is necessary – all I'm saying is don't actively go out and seek trouble until you and your team are absolutely completely and utterly ready to take back the world from those undead freaks (or until you need to nip out and get some new batteries for your iPod).

If there is a minor breach to your safe house (one or two zombies) then they will be easy to dispose of and the area easy to secure in a relatively short period of time.

If, however, you are attacked by a horde it will be safer to hide and wait for them to rampage through and on to the next meal rather than attempt to defend yourself against them all. This is why it's a good idea to have a hiding place with a few days' supplies ready in advance. It could be the attic or the cellar, or it could quite easily be under the bed or in a wardrobe. Obviously these last two choices aren't as comfortable as the first two – but they will be just as effective. Zombies are stupid so as long as you get to your hiding spot before the zombie sees you, they will not think to open a wardrobe door or bend down to look under a bed. It may be aware you are in the vicinity due to its sense of smell (if it does indeed still operate this sense), but it won't have the cognitive power to actually look for you. It will roam about for a bit and then it will eventually leave in search of the next meal.

If you do decide to use one of these simple hiding techniques, don't become cocky. A zombie will still hear you if you chant 'You can't see me! Ner Ner!' and will most likely throw the bed out of the way or smash the wardrobe to pieces. This plan, like most others, is also not foolproof, and should you be under the bed and the zombie falls over he will spot you. Or if your wardrobe was one of those cheap Ikea knockoffs it may collapse around you when you get in (I think you'll find it says in the instruction manual for most DIY wardrobes that they are not built for a person to live in). So although the option exists for you to hide in these places, we recommend going the extra mile and preparing somewhere a little more substantial.

HORDE

The noun that collectively describes a large unspecific amount of zombies all in the same place at the same time. This is by no use a definitive term and can be broken down into sub-segments.

You can use these terms specifically, although the word 'horde' is generally accepted when it is difficult to count just how many zombies are in one region at the same time.

Collective Terms for Zombies

A zombie	1 zombie
A couple of zombies	2 zombies
A few zombies	3 zombies
A host of zombies	4 – 15 zombies
A swarm of zombies	16 – 30 zombies
A throng of zombies	31 – 60 zombies
A thong of zombies	31 – 60 zombies in their pants
An assemblage of zombies	61 – 80 zombies
A coterie of zombies	81 – 100 zombies
A jonty beavan of zombies	over 100 zombies

HOSPITAL

See **Panic Zone**

HUMAN REMAINS

Not really a nice thing to think about, but as some of you may be aware, there is the possibility that people will *die* during a zombie apocalypse, and although there are cases where these dead bodies will rise again, eventually, once you've done your brain-destroying business, there will be a corpse that has to be dealt with.

There may be some of you that believe that once a corpse is down for good it is no longer a threat and can be left to rot in the streets as you continue on your merry way. Consider, though, several facts. If this is a viral or genetic zombie outbreak the infection that causes zombification could still be present in the inert body, meaning that anyone who comes into contact with it will become infected. Also, prior to being transformed into a member of the shambling undead, this creature was actually a human just like you. Do they really deserve to have their body left in the middle of the street for feral animals to gnaw on and maggots and flies to live in?

That was a trick question – of course they should be left there! Don't tell me you had started to show a little compassion at this stage? We've already ascertained that we should be selfish towards the living, so why on earth should we really give a rat's patootie about a pile of degrading meat and bones? Let the blighter rot!

There is still the option of infection to consider, though – and the only way to deal with that is through fire, corrosive substances or concrete. Burial is not an option because then you would have to come in close contact with the body (you may already have come in close contact with the body during battle in which case, oops. Hand-to-hand fighting with zombies isn't really a clever thing to do). The body must be destroyed or inaccessible to any other survivors to avoid the zombie virus spreading any further.

Concrete can be a time-consuming affair what with having to mix it up and wait for it to dry, and unless you have killed the zombie in a DIY centre you are unlikely to want to lug bags of cement across town just to set a corpse in stone.

Corrosive substances are the better option, but they are notoriously difficult to come by – especially the level of substance you require to dissolve an entire body at any great speed. So that just leaves fire. Fire is the easiest and most convenient way of disposing of a body, but it is also the most dangerous as the smoke will likely attract zombies to the location of the bonfire and the flames may get out of control and cause major destruction in the particular area of town you are in. Your choices are rather limited, though. The best option is to prepare for a quick retreat, cremate the body and just keep your fingers crossed that it won't burn down half the city (although the great fire of London in 1666 did help to eradicate the great plague of the time so who knows, you may be doing the world a favour).

Should you have ended up with a corpse inside your very own safe house due to some strange twist of fate (home invasion or a team member transforming), unless you have concrete or corrosive substances in your house, then presume your location has been compromised and go and find somewhere else to stay. You cannot set fire to a corpse in the middle of your own home. If you are trapped inside due to zombie hordes then find some way to keep the body away from other survivors by locking off the room the corpse is in.

Of course there are situations in battle (e.g. when you have to make a hasty retreat) where you will be incapable of destroying the bodies, so don't feel too bad if you leave a pile of corpses in your wake. At the end of the day it may not even be a viral or genetic zombie virus anyway, meaning that the corpses aren't harmful to anyone. In which case, if you do have the time you should do what any thoughtful, compassionate human being would do in this situation and give them a decent burial. Nah. I'm joking again. You should loot the body of anything valuable and then be on your way to the next corpse (after spitting on it first).

HUNDRED

I was just looking through the Collins pocket dictionary (in colour) and do you know what the definition of a hundred is? 'Ten times ten'. Why not 'twenty times five' or 'twenty-five times four' or 'a hundred times one' or 'forty-seven times 2.1276595'.

That's all I have to say on the matter. It just interested me. There is no real relevance to the term a hundred in zombie training apart from the fact that a hundredweight is 112 lbs which might come in handy. Oh, and over a hundred zombies is classed as a jonty beavan of Zombies.

HUNGER

This is something you may have to get used to during a zombie apocalypse as food will become scarce and difficult to come by. Supermarkets and food stores rank high on the scale of 'Panic Zones' (see **Panic Zones**) and will either have been looted very early on in the apocalypse or be overrun by the shambling undead. So, what do you do? Well, you can't starve to death, as death will severely scupper your chances of survival, so you have two choices. Firstly, you can stock up now with tinned food that is liable to last a long time without going out of date. Then you will have a designated supply that will last the siege during the early days of the apocalypse before the undead settle down a bit and start to wander the planet aimlessly.

If that seems a little boring for your taste (being prepared often can be a little boring) then think of the alternative where you have no food and have to eat your shoes, pot plants and Michael Bublé CD collection. Also think about the sense of satisfaction you will get from saying 'told you so' to the naysayers and doubters who pooh-poohed your stockpiling of beans and soup. Whilst you're at home enjoying a good meal they'll be chowing down on huarache sandals, rhododendrons and *Crazy Love*. Hmm – the sweet taste of always being right... (Please note that the taste of 'always being right' will not stop you from starving to death.)

ID

Not the 2007 album by Polish songstress Anna Maria Jopek (although we're sure finishing 11th in the Eurovision Song Contest would qualify you quite highly enough to survive a zombie apocalypse – if you have suffered the hardship of performing at Eurovision you can pretty much be guaranteed to survive anything.) Today we shall be discussing the id as part of the human psyche.

According to Freud in his *New Introductory Lectures on Psychoanalysis* in 1933, the id is 'the dark, inaccessible part of our personality, what little we know of it we have learnt from our study of the dream-work and of the construction of neurotic symptoms, and most of this is of a negative character and can be described only as a contrast to the ego. We all approach the id with analogies: we call it a chaos, a cauldron full of seething excitations... It is filled with energy reaching it from the instincts, but it has no organisation, produces no collective will, but only a striving to bring about the satisfaction of the instinctual needs subject to the observance of the pleasue principle.'

In layman's terms it is the crazy bit of our personality. The id is responsible for our basic drives such as food, water, sex, etc. It is essentially our biological instincts that are quashed by social and moral restraints. Put simply, who hasn't wished they could just get up and walk round to the call centre and stab that cold caller in the head when they rang just as you were about to sit down to dinner? The reason you don't do it? Because morally you know it's wrong and society would condemn you and put you in prison (also call centres hide their numbers so you wouldn't be able to find them anyway). But the instinct is there to cause damage to the caller as your sprouts go cold – this is your id in action.

When the apocalypse occurs, society will crumble around you and moral guidelines will become more blurred so your id will be allowed to run somewhat freer than it usually does. This is no bad thing as it will mean that you are allowing your subconscious to react to what your body needs in order to survive. Be careful, though. The id is disorganised and illogical. In some respects it is quite primal and if allowed to take control of your personality completely will turn you into something of a psycho. As a zombie-killing machine this will be most effective, but when dealing with other survivors it might not go down so well if you beat them to death in order to get their cornflakes.

Of course, how we apply the id to individuals can vary from case to case and in a zombie apocalypse we will all act and react in different ways. Some of us will retain our sense of moral values and community, whilst others will decide that they want to go completely nuts. During training it is marginally important to look at how our own psychology will affect our conduct and ultimately our chances of survival – maybe by booking occasional sessions with a psychotherapist to ensure we remain balanced and focused, but then there are those who believe it is a load of old tosh and that psychiatry is the last tool we will need in the quest to survive.

If that is the case then we in no way encourage you to follow a thorough personal psychological analysis of your own id. However, should you fall foul of a zombie attack due to a buried Oedipal complex deep within your own subconscious, don't blame me.

IGLOO

One popular theory maintains that zombies will not be able to cope with severely low temperatures and will freeze (note that this will not kill them; they will merely freeze solid until they are defrosted and then will continue as normal once they have thawed out. For further info see **Temperature**). So, regarding survival it may not be a bad idea to head somewhere that has temperatures lower than -20°C. Surviving in these conditions will have its own problems, but with a lack of zombies to contend with in the snow-covered poles it is not really my concern how you get on once you've made the decision to go there.

I will, however, point out that the best form of abode in an area covered with snow and ice is an igloo. The construction material is easily accessible, and the igloos themselves are warm and reliably strong (a correctly constructed igloo can hold the weight of a person standing on top). For further information on building these structures I suggest watching *Nanook of the North*.

It is also worth pointing out that although an igloo is a perfect abode when in a frozen wasteland, we would not recommend attempting to build one in any other locale. Even if you are holed up in the freezer department of Farmfoods. It will be a waste of time and water.

IKEA

Oh, for those halcyon days of having a solid oak desk to barricade a door with. Now, due to mass consumerism and a flat-pack culture, the very company we revere for its designer simplicity may be our downfall, due to substandard barricades. The interior design and decoration gods of Sweden cannot be held completely to blame, though. Look me in the eye and tell me you always read the instructions on how to put your furniture together properly. Really? Really?! So you're telling me that there's never one screw left over that you're not quite sure where it goes so you just leave it out! Do you realise that by doing this you may have condemned yourself to death? That when you place your bookshelf against the door, that missing screw could be the difference between a solid barricade or the whole thing collapsing on itself! So, in fact, it's not Ikea's fault at all – it's your shoddy workmanship!

Although on the other hand, furnishing your house in Ikea furniture could actually be quite handy. Because it is all flat pack, it means that you could transport it all with you when you need to move on to the next place. Beds, sofas, desks, baths. Just unscrew them all, stick them in a suitcase and away you go. It may also be of interest to know that Ikea also sell flat-pack housing ('tis true) so, why bother moving your furniture when you can move your whole house? If the zombie apocalypse begins, just grab your power drill, unscrew the whole thing, stick it on the back of your bike and peddle off into the hills where you can find a nice, zombie-free, secluded spot and rebuild again.

In fact, we could be looking at our zombie survival techniques in completely the wrong way by allowing the army and government to research new weapons. We should actually be asking Ikea to do it! A flat-pack tank stored in your cupboard under the stairs could be invaluable. Likewise, a flat-pack missile launcher under the sink, or a flat-pack bomb shelter stored in the attic to be dragged out at the appropriate time.

Of course, in the case of these items, we would recommend that you DO read the instructions correctly as you want to make sure that the gun's pointing the right way on the flat-pack tank – and who knows the consequences of a missing screw on a missile launcher?

INFECTION

Infection by a zombie virus is primarily through a bite from another infected person; do not discount the fact that the infection may be transmitted in other ways, though. Either as an airborne virus, in water, through blood, touch, toilet seats, kissing or phone sex. Until you receive definitive intelligence on how infection is caused, remain cautious.

INSANITY

It is a real shame, but with all the death, destruction, chaos and flesh-eating that's going on during the apocalypse there will be some people whose minds won't be able to cope. That little elastic band in their psyche that holds it all together will go ping and snap, sending them spiralling into a world of insanity. This will make them neither use nor ornament in the battle against the undead.

You may be able to halt the progression of some people's mental breakdown by following the counselling advice laid out in the counselling segment. Those who are beyond help will either need to be disposed of swiftly or used as a distraction to facilitate your own escape. Here are a few examples of the insanity you may encounter during a zombie apocalypse:

It's not happening

This form of insanity may seem quite mild, but it is highly dangerous as the person suffering believes that life is continuing as normal. Therefore, they will happily leave doors wide open, they will play live music and they will treat members of the undead like normal human beings and invite them in for tea and crumpets. When this form of insanity manifests itself, the person suffering is not always beyond redemption and you may be able to snap them out of their trance. If you cannot then just ask them to nip down the newsagents and pick you up twenty Bensons. It's unlikely you'll ever see them again – and if you do, you'll have fags. Bonus!

The screamy shouter

Complete bellowing madness with all the wailing, moaning, thrashing and spitting that you would imagine would occur when total breakdown hits. The stress of the situation will force the sufferer to attempt to expel some of the tension they are feeling through screaming very loudly and foaming at the mouth. It is not too hard to see why it would be dangerous to have a screamer alongside you in an apocalyptic situation. Once this level of lunacy has been reached electrotherapy and a straight jacket is what's needed and you won't have time for that. Hit them with a spade. Hard.

Catatonia

It would be lovely to have Cerys Matthews with you when the undead rise. She could sing you to sleep at night with her haunting rendition of 'Mulder and Sculley'. Unfortunately we're talking about a different kind of catatonia. The kind where the sufferer will exhibit complete loss of motor functions and show ignorance of any external stimuli. Depending on the level of the problem this could come in fits and starts and manifest as a series of blackouts for the patient, or it could be constant. Either way, the last thing you need during battle is for the person fighting by your side to suddenly go catatonic.

Killing a catatonic person is not always your only option, though. Depending on the level of rigidity in their body when they lose motor function, it may be possible to use them as part of a barricade, a battering ram or a draught excluder, should the wind be creeping in under your door.

I am Spartacus

The belief that they are someone else completely can sometimes overcome a person, meaning that they themselves do not have to cope with the situation they are in. This could be manifested as multiple personalities or with the sufferer believing they are Admiral Lord Nelson, the Queen, Spartacus or Buck Rogers.

If they believe that they are someone relatively normal then this is sometimes absolutely no problem to deal with as you would treat them like any other person who you were attempting to survive with. The difficulties occur if they believe that they are imbued with super powers or happen to have become God. In this case, you need to get rid of them as soon as possible before they open the door to your safe house believing that they can keep everyone safe. It won't be too difficult to rid yourself of the problem. Just tell them to go and fly off the roof or use their cloak of invisibility to pass unseen through a horde, or make the zombie masses part like Moses did with the Red Sea. Either way, you can use their supposed power to be their ultimate downfall.

Undead-lover

These weirdos must have made some really bad relationship decisions in the past, because when the dead rise they will see them as some kind of holy thing to be worshipped and adored. The only thing you have to worry about with these idiots is that they close the door on their way out to give their dearest undead a hug and get themselves killed.

Chomper

The worst form of insanity is if someone actually believes they are a zombie when they are not; that by becoming their nemesis they will become safe from it. This is in no way similar to emulation (see **Emulation**). They will not just pretend to be a zombie; they will become a zombie just without being dead. They will try and bite you and they will seem impervious to pain (their mental state will cause them to block their pain receptor. They will however be affected eventually – the human body can only take so much. The plus side to this is, unlike real zombies, you don't have to go for the head shot and they will be disposed of quite easily, leaving you to carry on living a life of quiet normality and battling the undead.

INNER CITY REDEVELOPMENT
AND ROAD PLANNING

'Quick, turn right now!'
'That won't get us out of the city!'
'It will! Trust me! Turn right!'

'Full right or bear right?'

'You missed it! Damn it!'

'It's OK, I'll go down here! Damn! Where did those bollards come from?'

'Reverse! Reverse!'

'It's one way!'

'It's a zombie apocalypse, it doesn't matter! Quick, cut down that alley!'

'This is a pedestrian area!'

'Turn right. Now!'

'But we need to be over the other side of town!'

'I know what I'm doing!'

'What the hell is that blocking the road?'

'It depicts the flourish of youth that lives within the life of us all.'

'It looks like a few hunks of rusted metal with a fibre optic light in it.'

'Cost the council three million pounds.'

'I shouldn't really run it over then.'

'Go down this road here.'

'But we've driven past that Starbucks three times now!'

'Turn right!'

'But we need to be over the other side of the canal!'

'Watch those speed bumps!'

'Who put those bollards there?'

'Oh screw this, I'm just going to get out and let the zombies eat me.'

INSECTS

Things to bear in mind regarding insects during a zombie apocalypse:

1) Mosquitoes, flies, lice etc. spread disease. Ensure you keep your safe house and your own body clean to stop the spread of disease.

2) Some insects aid in decomposition. Something that is generally overlooked by popular media in the depiction of the undead is that they will most likely be surrounded by flies and will have other insects living in or on them. Zombies are rotting flesh and this will attract some insects to them. It is unlikely that insects will be prey to zombies and as zombies don't feel pain, they will not try and stop the infestation of our six-legged friends. The insects then eat the rotting flesh and, although it is a time-consuming way to await the end of the apocalypse, they will ultimately kill the zombies. (A disturbing side effect to this rather positive thought is that the flies who eat the zombie flesh may then be able to transmit the virus.)

3) Some insects make things. Bees make honey. Honey tastes nice. Yum. Silk worms make something too – it eludes me exactly what at the moment.

4) You can eat insects – only some of them, mind, so don't just go and stick your head in a termite mound and hope for the best. Amongst those that are tried and tested are Green Thai Crickets, Toasted Leafcutter Ants and Chocolate Covered Giant Ants – I'm not too sure to which area chocolate-covered ants

are indigenous, but I'm sure further research on the intcrwcb will reveal where to find them.

5) Some insects could survive a nuclear explosion (cockroaches can't, that's an urban legend – but fruit flies could). With that in mind, it may be a good idea to make yourself a suit out of fruit flies. This will keep you safe should the authorities decide to nuke your area in order to destroy the zombie menace.

6) Without the correct predators to control population, some species could potentially reproduce so quickly that they could literally bury the whole world in one season. Not really sure there's anything you could do about that.

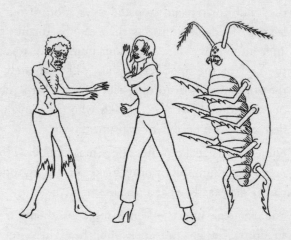

INSTANT REACTION

What's the first thing you should do on hearing of a zombie apocalypse? Get to your loved ones? Grab a weapon and start fighting? Jump off a building? Set your Sky+ to record all the programmes you might miss? Tidy your room? No. No. No. Possibly. No! The first thing you should do is get yourself secure.

That doesn't mean you need to move to the place that you had designated as a safe house in your zombie plan. What it means is that you need to get yourself locked into any building (apart from **Panic Zones**) and barricade the doors as quickly as you can. At this stage don't worry about supplies or weapons. There may be things within the building you have chosen that can be utilised should the need arise. But if you have secured yourself correctly then the need shouldn't arise for weapons and you shouldn't have to wait too long before you can venture out and look for food.

The reason for this action is simple. As soon as the apocalypse begins all hell will break loose: there will be panic on the streets, people won't know what's going on, and the place will become a war zone. With so much mayhem it will be difficult to keep focused and keep yourself safe. By distancing yourself from the chaos and ensuring the building you have chosen is correctly secured, you are effectively biding your time until the initial panic is over. This won't take as long as you think – either the authorities will gain control or the dead will win. Either way you will reach the other side of the initial outbreak alive.

Unlike a conventional war, the dead won't start searching house to house. Once the carnage is over they will become docile and start wandering around aimlessly. Once they have begun this process (after the majority of the living are dead or reanimated) that is when you can put your survival plan into action and head for your designated safe house.

INSURANCE

Although a cursory search of the Internet only reveals hoax and comedy versions of insurance cover in the event of a zombie apocalypse, this is not a matter to take lightly. If you feel it necessary (and should you also believe that the financial stability of the world's currencies – and the insurance company – will survive through the apocalypse), then by all means take out a policy. Many high-profile insurance firms have specialist departments that deal with out of the ordinary requests, including the insurance of celebrity body parts and unique highly expensive items, so insurance against a zombie apocalypse must be within the realms of possibility.

At the moment one is able to purchase insurance against alien abduction and to also double the payout should you become pregnant with an alien baby during the abduction (available to both men and women), so I imagine it won't be long before some forward-thinking insurance company comes up with the idea of zombie insurance. When they do though, we'll be the ones who come out laughing. Alien abduction insurance will never be cashed in, but a zombie apocalypse is bound to happen.

INTERFERONS

Interferons (IFNs) are natural cell-signalling proteins produced by the cells of the immune system of most vertebrates in response to challenges such as viruses, parasites and tumour cells. Interferons belong to the large class of glycoproteins known as cytokines. They are produced by a wide variety of cells in response to the presence of double-stranded RNA, a key indicator of viral infection. Interferons assist the immune response by inhibiting viral replication within host cells, activating natural killer cells and macrophages, increasing antigen presentation to lymphocytes, and inducing the resistance of host cells to viral infection.

But I don't know why you'd be interested in that because THERE IS NO CURE! How many times do I have to tell you? Stop holding on to the possibility that you might be immune! You're not! Nobody is! Why? Because there is no cure!

INTERNET

Due to the continuing computerisation of the world and the fact that a lot of our day-to-day amenities no longer need constant human supervision in order to operate, I'm sure that you'll all be pleased to know that the Internet should stay up and running a fair way into the apocalypse. And you should have continued access to it as long as your electricity holds out or you don't need to use your laptop to barricade a door.

There will, of course, be certain sites that will be of use and those that won't. To help get your priorities straight let's have a look at some of them.

Facebook

When used correctly Facebook can be an excellent way of increasing your survivalist contacts worldwide so that you can monitor the possibility of zombie outbreaks and share survival tips with a prepared global community. Don't become distracted by the some of the other wonders that this social networking site has to offer, though (poking people, building a farm, running a mafia gang or joining any groups that promise to show you pictures that will make you either LOL, ROFL, PMSL or LKAOPSBQG) as it will seriously eat into your training time.

RECOMMENDED GROUPS ON FACEBOOK:

- Zombie Apocalypse Preparation

- You've Got Dead On You

- The Hardest Part of a Zombie Apocalypse Will Be Pretending I'm Not Excited

- How to Survive a Zombie Apocalypse*

That last one is ours – you can talk to me direct on that one.

YouTube

Amateur filmmakers ahoy! Do not waste your time looking on YouTube for any useful information about the apocalypse. It will be inundated with undergraduate media studies students uploading grainy footage of themselves snivelling into the camera in night vision about how scared they are. They'll believe this to be a true and honest depiction of the unadulterated horror that the world is enduring. All in the hope that after the apocalypse, should they survive, their opus will be picked up for a Best Documentary Award at Cannes.

The best you can hope for is that while they're being self-obsessed about the lighting, one of the undead will lumber up behind them and chew off an ear – now that would be entertainment.

eBay

The place to get anything! Weapons, fuel, survival gear and this book (probably for less than what you paid for it in the shops). Problem is, I'm not sure that the postal service will be running at 100% efficiency during the apocalypse so it may be as well to ensure that if you do buy anything you get the seller to guarantee personal delivery within 24 hours (even if it is from abroad). If they don't then threaten to leave negative feedback. That'll hurt them.

Twitter

An excellent way to find out if your loved ones and major celebrities are alive and well. We suggest updating your Twitter at least every three minutes with the statement 'I'm Still Alive' up until the point you are not (it won't be necessary to update your Twitter once you are no longer alive).

Porn sites

Bear this in mind. Once the apocalypse has been going on for a few months and there are fewer clean, living humans around, and the electricity has finally switched off so neither your computer or your TV works, where are you going to get your kicks, eh? Get onto those sites now and get that printer working on overtime!

JESUS

I do not wish to offend anyone, so I thought it best to take this opportunity to clear up a few things about the son of God and the rumours about him being a member of the undead.

Based on the fact that Jesus rose from the dead, it has been claimed that he is, in fact, a zombie. I would like to make it clear right now, in order to stop further speculation and the sullying of this religious icon's character, that Jesus was *not* a zombie. OK?

Granted, according to the bible he rose from the dead – but once risen, he didn't go and chew on Mary Magdalene, did he? No. Did he shamble around aimlessly moaning, groaning and rotting? No! He continued to speak and act like a normal human being. It is just childish to associate a man, whom many people believe in so faithfully, with a wandering, mindless corpse just because he demonstrated one attribute of the zombie myth. Ozzy Osborne shambles around and makes incoherent grunts and that doesn't make him a zombie, does it? Zombies are heinous, nasty creatures and suggesting that Jesus may have been one is just wrong. It's much more likely that Jesus was a vampire.

JOGGING

Many times I've looked out of my window over the park and thought to myself: why are those people running really slowly? What purpose does it serve? It doesn't get you anywhere any quicker than a fast stride and you seem to have to wear very small shorts or velour to do it.

Then it occurred to me that these people might be on to

something. You see, running can be very tiring and walking sometimes just doesn't cut it when you want to get somewhere quickly. This is where jogging comes in.

When the dead rise they will be slow (see **Speed**), so why waste your energy running away from them at full pelt waving your arms and screaming like a girl. They can muster up no more than a shamble so why should you bother putting in the effort to get away quickly? It's not as if the zombie is going to think to himself: 'Oh! Look at him go! I'm not going to bother chasing after that one. He's waaaaaaaay too fast for me. Oh, look! There's a girl in heels – she's a better prospect.'

A zombie will go for whichever prey is nearest, so whether you're running, skipping or moonwalking away he's still going to be heading in your direction until you get yourself locked up in your safe house.

Jogging is the perfect way to get there. At a slow pace it keeps you a safe distance ahead of your pursuer, and hopefully allows you to get out of his line of sight and into your safe house unseen. And you can do this without tiring yourself out in case of a surprise attack from more zombies coming from another direction.

JOURNAL

It may be very useful to keep a journal once the apocalypse begins. But before you lick the end of your quill and begin to pen your innermost thoughts and fears, please note that I am not suggesting you become the Anne Frank of the zombie apocalypse. The truth is that no one really cares about anyone else's innermost thoughts. Be honest. Do you really give a hoot about what any of your friends are feeling deep down? When you occasionally catch them with a sad and wistful look in their eyes do you honestly wonder what dark thoughts are swooping around the depths of their soul? No. You don't. You'd much prefer that everyone was talking about you.

So, sorry to burst your bubble, but no one really cares how you felt when you killed your first zombie, or discovered that your Uncle Nancy was infected or when you saw your first badger. Most of them will have been through those experiences themselves. You are, after all, *survivors*. Instead, your journal should be succinct and to the point. It should detail the areas you've been scavenging in, what supplies you have, how many zombies you have killed and where you have seen the hordes massing. The kind of thing that would be useful should you come into contact with other survivors or should you die and need to pass the information on.

Look upon your journal as a constant battle plan and a guide to plan your campaigns. If your groups go on separate scavenging missions you will be able to keep track of who got what from where and who spotted which dead in which areas. This will save your team from going on wasted trips back to areas that have been bled dry of supplies and it will also allow you to track the direction of the zombie migration in order to avoid them.

The information in your journal may mean the difference between life and death when your team is depleted and the days are running into each other and tiredness is setting in. So don't waste time and space drawing daisies in the margins and smiley faces as dots for your *i*s.

JUMPING

Jumping is very much an overlooked skill in the art of survival; however, it can turn out to be a very useful skill to have. Look at the influence this pure act of lifting two feet off the ground at the same time has had on us over the years. Girls Aloud implored us to 'Jump for their love' and Kris Kross saw the potential to reach millions with their simple message of 'Jump, jump, jump, jump, jump, jump, jump.' Leo told us that if we jumped, he'd jump and in 2007 Patrick Swayze and Martine McCutcheon gave us a tense psychological drama about anti-Semitism and the unjust murder trial of a young Jew in a film entitled...you guessed it – 'Jump'!

So, how do we learn to jump properly? Well, first let's start with something simple: the stationary jump (this is jumping when standing still and not jumping over a pile of pencils, rulers and an A4 folder). Here's how we do it:

1) Quickly raise both feet off the floor.
2) Return feet to floor.

There are two important issues to bear in mind when carrying out this simple procedure. Firstly, don't fall over, and secondly don't forget to carry out point 2, as without point two you would be levitating – which, although vastly more impressive than jumping, may cause other survivors to treat you as if you were possessed and burn you at the stake.

Once you have mastered the stationary jump you will be able to reach shelves that were previously too high, avoid a low sweeping attack from a member of the undead and confidently hold your own in a mosh pit.

The next step up, once the stationary jump is mastered, is the 'travelling jump' (jumping over things like a hole or rooftops).

Unfortunately, due to space restrictions we won't be able to go into that today, but much can be learnt about the art of jumping from the interweb and we urge you to carry on bettering yourself in this art, incorporating such gems as the 'star jump', 'wolf jump', 'straddle jump' and 'ring' (no jump on the end of that, but it's still a jump – trust me, I'm a doctor).

Eventually, with all these jumps in your repertoire you may even be able to master the art of 'parkour' which although sounds a bit French is actually quite impressive and will allow you to jump around a council estate wearing baggy jeans and a baseball cap – a useful skill if ever there was one.

KAMIKAZE

Maybe I should have mentioned this earlier, but if you're planning on strapping explosives to yourself and running into the middle of a horde of zombies, it somewhat defeats the art of surviving. As does crashing a plane into a horde of zombies, driving a burning oil tanker off a cliff into a horde of zombies and running into a horde of zombies shouting 'You're all smelly girls!' armed with nothing but a bendy straw. If that was your plan from the offset then you've really wasted your money buying this book.

KANGAROO

For those who think it's possible, you cannot hide in the pouch of a kangaroo. You won't fit, the zombies will still get you and the kangaroo probably won't be best pleased either.

KARMA

Do you believe in karma? The theory of what goes around comes around? Bad things happen to bad people? Consider this: in speculative projections it is thought that if a zombie apocalypse occurs and the virus is transmitted by bite only, 92% of the population of the UK will be dead or reanimated within a week. Now surely that amount of people can't have done that much wrong? If you were a mass murderer or rapist then I can understand that Karma would be shaking his head at you and cooking up some pretty darn special punishment to sneak up and bite you in the ass – and becoming a rotting, animated corpse might just fit that bill. But then, surely 56,600,000 folks can't have been naughty enough to deserve that kind of punishment.

At the moment the idea goes that if you steal a pen from work, you might drop 20p under a shop counter and be unable to retrieve it. And thus the cosmic balance is restored and the universe is in order again. The bigger the crime, the bigger the consequence. I have to say, I wouldn't like to be a claims assessor sitting in the Karma Corporations head office in this day and age. With so many misdemeanors occurring it must be hard to keep everything aligned, which is probably why the zombie apocalypse is going to occur in the first place. Some trainee karma operator or member of middle management having a mid-life crisis is going to flick a switch that is going to rain down punishment on the whole population irrespective of what the crime is. So, anyone who has done anything mildly spankworthy will become a walking corpse. This leaves us with two possible morals to the story:

1) If you do anything bad, from eating the last hobnob to poking a nun in the eye with a pencil, you will become a zombie due to karmic resolution, or

2) If you don't believe in karma then none of this will happen because not believing in something means it doesn't exist and then you can just ignore it and get on with your biscuit-stealing and nun-poking.

Either way it's all a bit too much to bear thinking about so I think I'm going to go and find a nice comfy kangaroo to have a lie down in.

KATANA

The melee weapon of melee weapons. Damn the machete! Throw down that spear! I spit on your chainsaw and ridicule your big pointy stick. Zombie survivalists the world over revel in the shiny loveliness of the Japanese beauty that is known as the katana. With a curved blade of over 60 cm and a squared guard and broad handle ideal for two-handed usage, it is renowned for its cutting ability almost to the level of mythological proportions. Kevin Costner was seen dropping a silk scarf over one in a sexy manner in *The Bodyguard* (if that doesn't make you want to rush out and buy one I don't know what will).

Also, it's illegal to own one in the UK due to an amendment to the Offensive Weapons Order of 2008, so unfortunately you'll just have to go back to using that big pointy stick. Or move to Japan.

KNITTING

You can make your own clothes and have two pointy sticks to use as weapons at the same time. What else needs to be said?

KNOTS

You've got a piece of rope – what possible use could it be? Well, you could use it to make a trip wire across a door, as a possible escape route out of an upstairs window, to attach your supplies to the back of your giraffe or just coil it up and wear it as a hat. The uses for rope are endless, but all of those applications will be less than successful if you don't know how to tie a decent knot.

Over the centuries people bored with stamp collecting have gone in for the far more thrilling study of knots, learning about both their practical and mathematical attributes. Now, we're not particularly bothered about the mathematical properties of the simple knot (it is unlikely that you will find much use for the equation $J = N - 2$ during a zombie apocalypse), but discovering the practical applications and learning to tie strong and effective knots that will hold under pressure could be the difference between you comfortably abseiling to safety down the side of a building or ending up as a mushy paste on the pavement below.

Here is a basic list of knots and their rudimentary uses which you may find handy during the apocalypse:

The Sheet Bend – Used for tying two similar-sized ropes together.

Double Sheet Bend – Used for tying two dissimilar-sized ropes together.

Truckers Hitch – Used to tighten a load and secure it.

Diamond Hitch – Used for loading pack animals.

Spanish Bowline – Used to hoist a person aloft.

Prusik Knot – Used for ascending a rope.

Buntline Hitch – Used for tying a rope to a pole.

Hitchline Bunt – Used for tying a pole to a rope.

Loftys Clump – Used for descending a rope into a pit of fire.

Crabcleft Man Knot – Used for dangling a piano over a large open space from a chandelier.

Drabcan Shamalyn Triple Dogger – Used for sealing Weetabix boxes.

Triple Whore-Maker Frumpline Staple Cran Boogle Knot – Used for attaching a rope to an elastic band that in turn is tied to the back of an articulated lorry that is currently hanging over the edge of a canyon in the south west of America whilst your sister sits at home listening to James Blunt on the radio whilst reading Proust.

LEARNING

Yes, that's what you're doing now. Learning all about how to survive a zombie apocalypse. Although the bigger question is, can a zombie learn to survive the coming human apocalypse? Are zombies capable of being taught? Now for those of you who are considering the idea of grabbing yourself a couple of undead, sticking them in silly hats and teaching them to dance, I'm going to stop you right there. Using zombies to add a new twist to your children's entertainment business is just not going to work – not unless you could at least get them to learn magic or some form of acrobatic trick, but even then I'd stick with making balloon animals if given the choice. The point is, though, that technically speaking, yes, zombies can learn. Any creature that is aware of its surroundings will eventually adapt to those surroundings over time.

Let's just make one thing clear from the offset – zombies will hold no memories of their past lives. They will not remember where they lived, who their friends were, what TV shows they liked or how to make an omelette. They will also not remember how to carry out simple everyday tasks like climbing ladders and using door handles to open doors.

But they will adapt to their surroundings. A zombie will be able to perceive when an object is solid and can thus not pass through it. Which is why we will not see zombies just walking willy-nilly into walls, trees and post boxes. To begin with, they will not know what glass is – and we may get a few chortle-worthy moments as a member of the undead goes shambling face first into a plate glass window. A zombie can also tell the difference between a member of the undead and a living survivor which is why they do not attack each other.

So, we can deduce from these few simple facts about the undead that they do have a sense of perception. And any creature with perception, no matter how simple, will adapt to its environment. After a few attempts at walking directly into shop windows, they will 'learn' what glass is and not attempt to do that anymore.

The positive side to this rather scary thought is that humans tend to learn a lot by trial and error. You wouldn't stick your hand in a fire because you know it would hurt. Because a zombie feels no pain it will never learn not to walk into fire.

Humans are also taught a great deal by other humans (either by witnessing others' mistakes or by teaching each other). Zombies are not a species that will socialise so there will be no sharing of information between them. They also reproduce in an unconventional way so will never pass on their teachings to new zombies.

Therefore, if we do destroy a zombie, the things it has 'learnt' will die with it. And every new zombie that comes along will have to start afresh walking into windows.

But do bear in mind that scientists still don't understand the inner workings of the human brain and they've been studying those for decades. So how can we ever hope to know what is going on inside the brain of the undead? If a zombie is left wandering the earth long enough – will it begin to understand more?

Everything evolves after time and there is no reason to think the undead will be an exception. After all, they learnt how to use weapons and adapt to their surroundings in *Land of the Dead*; in *Cell* they began using previously defunct parts of their brains to harness psychic powers, including levitation and hypnosis; and they learnt the beauty of rising to the occasion, the importance of seizing a special opportunity, and the special empowerment achieved through respect for the dignity of others in *The Princess Diaries...* Or that may have been Anne Hathaway? Anyway, this is why it is imperative that we do not attempt to close ourselves off from the hordes or attempt to live a life alongside them. Who knows what they could learn and ultimately become? And then we would have real problems on our hands. Fighting a zombie that felt no pain but had a plan! No! Whatever you do, once you have the means you must ensure that every last zombie is put down for good! Because once they start to show signs of sentience you will have your greatest enemy yet to face: tree-hugging Liberals fighting for the Rights of the Undead. And THAT really doesn't bear thinking about.

LORRAINE KELLY

Forget Chuck Norris, Jean Claude Van Damme, Arnie and Bruce Lee, this mistress of morning television is the perfect person to have around in the apocalypse. Her life as a reporter has meant she has amassed a gargantuan amount of information that pertains to all walks of life. This could come in handy once civilisation starts to break down. For instance, she has filmed her own fitness videos, meaning that she is in peak physical condition; during her early morning shows on Sky, episodes of *ER* were shown meaning that she will have learnt how to carry out all manner of surgical procedures that could help significantly when the apocalypse begins (especially if a helicopter falls on you). She is also used to functioning on very few hours of sleep, all the while balancing family life with show business extravagance and early morning broadcasts. Compared to all that, dealing with midnight attacks from the undead will be a doddle.

She is also always so upbeat and jolly that she would be the perfect companion to have along for the journey to keep up the team morale. She'll regale you with fascinating tales of her life –

releasing cheetahs into the wilds of Namibia or guest-hosting *The Paul O'Grady Show*. Also, as a result of being involved in secret government testing, she can hear any sound regardless of distance, volume or frequency, is imbued with great strength and can move up to speeds of over 200mph (that last bit might actually be the bionic woman, but you never know with Lorraine).

LOVE

All you need is love.

No. All you need is three years' worth of supplies within a steel-walled and heavily secured safe house that has running water and electricity – along with a variety of effective weapons. Love is highly overrated in survival situations. Will love build a bridge? Not as efficiently as a team of construction operatives with pneumatic tools.

MAGIC

The apocalypse is upon us! Quick, to King's Cross and all aboard the train for Hogwarts! Harry will save us!

I hate to break it to you at this point, guys, but there is no Hogwarts and there is no Harry Potter; they're both actually just a little bit fictional.

However, I am loath to admit that there is the very slight possibility of some form of magic being involved in the raising of the dead. This is actually only very very very very very very slight and is only worth mentioning just briefly due to how very very slight the possibility may be (I think I mentioned it was slight).

If our undead plague is down to Supernatural Zombies (see **Classification**) then there could be the (slight) possibility that someone has got their necromancy mojo on and has decided to cast some all-powerful spell to enable the dead to walk the earth. Now, the reason that I say that this is only a slight possibility (I think I did mention that it was slight) is because *it hasn't happened yet*. If there was some incantation that made corpses walk then you'd think one of the millions of power-crazed loons and unstable megalomaniacs who inhabit this little planet of ours would have been unable to resist the temptation to unleash all hell upon mankind and make themselves the emperor of Earth.

Also, a cursory glance through the *Encyclopedia of Spells* and a quick Google of 'spells to raise the dead' reveals nothing (although apparently you can find love by using an old sock and some pubic hair). So either there isn't a spell to raise the dead or those in the know ain't talking and are guarding this immense power with their lives. Either way, this means the possibility of using magic to raise the dead is very slight. Very slight. Very, very slight. I don't know if I mentioned it's slight. Very.

MARTIAL ARTS

Everybody was kung-fu fighting. Ha! Hu cha! So says Carl Douglas, and if he is to be believed they were also fast as lightning (*ha, hu cha!*), but how useful will being a master in the martial arts be during a zombie apocalypse? Well, in some cases, good. In some cases, bad. Isn't that always the case?

Contrary to popular belief, the term 'martial arts' does not just refer to any Eastern form of fighting technique but more specifically to any discipline in the form of combat and hand-to-hand warfare (Mars is the God of War – hence *mar*tial arts), including boxing and fencing. So is it handy to have one, or some, or all of the different forms of martial arts in your skill set?

Yes, having the discipline to learn these arts certainly shows that you will have an aptitude for survival and will also, no doubt, have greater physical stamina because of it. But let us not forget how a zombie is destroyed. That's right, you need to eliminate the brain. So, although hand-to-hand combat may be an asset when attempting to keep an attacking corpse at bay it's not really going to cut the mustard when it comes to smushing the brain.

Now, I'm sure there are those martial artists out there who assure me that they could crush a zombie's skull with their bare hands – after all, we've seen little Japanese men chop through six-foot blocks of concrete before so I've no doubt it's possible. But please, a brain is squishy and messy. Do you really want to drive your bare hand, with force, into a brain? The mess will go all over the place – and it's unlikely you'll have running water to clean up with afterwards.

Besides the mess, it's not actually very safe either. The brain is in the head which is quite near the mouth, and the last thing you want to do is get bitten. But if you're waving your hand around near a zombie's face then that could very well be what happens. Even if your knuckle nicks the old dead boy's tooth whilst you smack him in the face, that's still a bite as far as we're concerned.

So, no matter how much you want to show off, close combat hand-to-hand is not recommended when dealing with zombies. The martial arts you need to utilise are the weapon-based ones: fencing or Gatka, Kendo, Eskrima or Jukendo. The majority of these disciplines focus on the use of bladed weaponry. However, once the discipline is mastered you can use any weapon within the structure of the art – be it golf clubs, baseball bats, standard lamps, small children or chairs. Each will be equally effective as a sword in both offensive and defensive manoeuvres.

> **NOTE:** This segment should not be confused with the *marital* arts which is really mummy and daddy code for sexy time. Go and get your kicks somewhere else, you freak.

MEDITATION

OK, so you need to relieve the obvious stress and tensions that will affect us all during the zombie apocalypse. I understand that. A calm and peaceful mind will do a much more effective job than a tightly wound and neurotic one. So, you just take all the time you need and close your eyes. That's it. Close your eyes and imagine yourself on a beautiful sun-drenched beach. You can hear the waves from the crystal blue waters lapping against the almost white sand as overhead the clouds just drift on slowly by and... No, just ignore that noise. That was just the house resettling. Yes, I know it sounded like footsteps outside the door but it was just a floorboard. Now, keep your eyes closed and let's get back to that beach... No, I didn't hear it again, now you're just imagining things. Keep your eyes closed and just drift, drift, imagine yourself floating... Yes, I'm sure there's nothing outside.

If there was a zombie outside do you think I'd have you sitting there in the lotus position with your eyes closed thinking about frigging palm trees and milky coconuts? No! I'd be yelling my head off trying to get you to help stop the thing ripping our limbs off and pulling our intestines out and drenching the walls and ceilings and floors with dark crimson blood and offal. So just close your frigging eyes and get back to the buggering beach!

OK! It's sunny, the clouds are drifting and the water's lapping at your feet! See? That didn't take long, did it? I'm sure you feel so much better now. Hang on, I'll just light one of these jasmine and peach candles to enhance the mood.

MEMORY

It's midnight and there's seemingly not a sound from the pavement (or so Elaine Paige would have us believe). The moon may not have lost her memory, but the undead certainly have. It is extremely important to remember that once a person becomes a zombie they will retain *no knowledge of their previous life as a human*. This means that they will not remember who they were, they will not remember who you are, and they will not remember how to use doors, guns, ladders, the TV remote, a Rubik's cube or be able to play Sudoku. You will not be able to appeal to their better nature or their human side because they will not have one. They will have forgotten it. They will have no memory. But (and it's a big but) BUT (sorry, there we go. That's a big but – the other but was just a regular sized but – maybe I should make my point more clearly) BUT (now that's a big but – and we like big buts, I cannot lie…) even though a zombie may not retain its human memories, it may have subliminal memories of certain aspects of its human existence. What do we mean by that? I shall explain…

The undead may be drawn to buildings or places that they visited on a regular basis – for example, shopping centres, places of work, pubs, and Taiwanese massage parlours. They won't know *why* they feel the need to go there, but through their subliminal thoughts they will be drawn to those places. This is also more likely if the place was known for drawing large crowds of people. The zombie's animal instinct will be telling it to go there as it knows there will be people to chomp on.

The undead may also show the tendency to repeat actions that they carried out repetitively whilst alive. If a zombie was a petrol pump attendant it may stand and remove and replace the pump from the stand repeatedly if it has nothing else to do. Again, it wouldn't know why it was doing it and it would soon stop if potential victims came along. The brain may retain these actions purely because they were carried out so often.

This finally leads us to the most disturbing thought – that maybe, just maybe, a zombie will recognise a loved one. Surely if they remember the way to the mall or how to use a petrol pump they will remember the person they've been married to for twenty years and they may go to a place they know that person would be?

Remember that although they'll go to the mall, they won't know why. They operate the petrol pump, but they don't know why. So, they may recognise your face, but they won't know why. All they will know is that their subliminal memory has led them to you and they will bite you. So much for twenty years of happy marriage.

MIGRATION

It all sounds very David Attenborough when you start talking about the migration habits of the undead. Perhaps you should imagine him reading this to you in his halting, whispery, husky tones – just to imbue the added weight of experience to the account. Or maybe you could imagine it being read by David Bellamy because he talks about migration too. Or if you've got an active imagination and you're in the mood, maybe you could picture some sultry sexpot reading it to you – Angelina Jolie or Brad Pitt. Maybe they're smearing you in chocolate sauce and honey whilst they're reading and maybe they're wearing a very tight thong or are completely naked. Maybe David Attenborough is there watching you and he's in a thong or naked too and he's narrating what's going on in his halting, whispery, husky tones to a live studio audience who are all naked as well. Smearing each other with large vats of chocolate sauce and honey.

Or we could just dispense with all of that and get on with the bit about migration.

The one driving force behind a zombie is a need to bite and

kill. But what do they do when there are no more folks to nibble on? Well...nothing really. If there is nothing for a zombie to attack it will do one of two things: it will either stand around and do nothing just swaying on the spot, slowly rotting away until something grabs its attention, or it will wander off in search of more survivors.

Zombies are not social creatures but they do have a tendency to group in hordes. It is not known why they do this but you can be assured it is unlikely to be anything to do with finding safety in numbers or because they're looking for a decent fourth to have a good game of bridge. It is more likely that if one zombie moves the others assume that it has got the scent of prey and they trust that they will be lead to some nice tasty human flesh. Just because zombies are seen to 'horde' that does not mean you should become complacent in seemingly abandoned areas. Some of the undead may have become distracted and left behind by the rest of the group and be standing loitering in a dark corner. Silently. Unmoving. Maybe naked. Just waiting to be aroused. But not by David Bellamy and a tub of chocolate sauce.

MOBILE TELEPHONE

Let's just get this clear. I'm talking about the plain old bog-standard mobile telephone. It doesn't matter that it has Internet access, inbuilt iTunes, a satnav, diaries, television, DVD player and the solution to all third-world debts. That is not a mobile telephone, that is the beginning of the Skynet revolution (see **Robots**). The focus today will be on the simple mobile telephone, an item which most of us in the Western world now possess.

Mobile networks are serviced by computer-run satellites so

it's likely they will still be up and running some way into the apocalypse. This means that as long as you keep your phone charged and topped up with credit (if that's the kind of contract you're on) then you should have a useful tool for discovering the whereabouts of members of your social and business network who have survived. You can then keep in touch with them and find out what's happening in other parts of the city/country/world whilst staying in the relative safety of your own sanctuary. It is also possible to carry on this communication network by text so you don't even have to vocalise and worry about the issue of making a noise that could attract the undead to your whereabouts. Unless... unless...you forgot to switch your phone to silent!

Those of you who have sat in a cinema or theatre and had to suffer the embarrassment of your mobile suddenly ringing during a performance have some understanding of the potential horror scenario. Remember all that tutting from the other members of the audience? Remember how some of them turned and glowered at you? Well, it will be just like that, except that you will also be ripped limb from limb.

Picture the scene. The apocalypse has begun and you've taken my advice to hide immediately. You have found a reasonable place to conceal yourself and don't envisage any of the dead finding you anytime soon. You'll just sit back and... Now imagine the Nokia theme tune blaring at top volume. You frantically grab for your pocket, but as is always the case with the damn thing being so small, you can't find it! Oh! Now it's tangled up in your keys and it's still ringing! Too late, the undead have been alerted to your whereabouts and whilst you've been preoccupied with trying to find your phone and turn it off they have descended upon your position. They grab you, bite you, tear you up and kill you – and all because you didn't turn your phone to silent. The added irony of it all? The call was from your network provider enquiring if you were happy with their service. You wouldn't know that though because they withheld their number. And didn't leave a message. I hate it when they do that.

MONEY

'He who has money can eat sherbet in hell'
Old Lebanese proverb

As we all know, when the apocalypse comes there will be no more room in hell, as that is why the dead are walking the earth and that's probably why they're hungry for flesh, because they can't get into hell to get at their sherbet so there's a sugar rush to fill. My point is (and I do have one) if you can't get into hell to get any of the lovely sherbet they have on offer then what is the use of having money when you're alive?

Of course, you need money now. How else would you be able to pay your bills, eat and purchase my next book (*Zombie Dictionary – The Other 36 Letters of the Alphabet You Didn't Know About*). But when the apocalypse is upon us money will become the least valuable commodity there is. So on hearing of the rising of the dead don't rush out to the nearest ATM, because all your cash will be good for is burning. During the apocalypse we will regress back into a life of bartering and trading goods so you need to make sure that you have the best goods to trade if you want to gain a position of power in this apocalyptic age.

Stop! Get off eBay right this second! When I say you need the best goods I don't mean a 72-inch plasma-screen TV. Again, as a status symbol for these current times it may be something that a fair few people covet, but when battling the undead and trying to survive some things will be slightly more important. Weapons, livestock, food, clean water – and what about those things that all the others have forgotten? Cigarettes? Alcohol? Toilet paper? Not exactly essentials, but can you imagine a world where you couldn't sit on a toilet with a bottle of brandy and a Regal King-size, safe in the knowledge that you would have a clean bottom once you finished? It is these things that you should begin to stockpile, along with your own personal supplies. These are the items that will allow you to purchase food, fuel and wives when you are running low.

Don't forget about life after the apocalypse either. Once all the zombies are dead and civilisation begins to rebuild itself, your stock-piled supplies will become more readily available to the general public so you need a back-up plan to ensure that your prosperity continues way into the future. This prosperity will lie with precious metals and gems. Gold and diamonds will still retain their value after the apocalypse as high-end bargaining chips purely due to their rarity.

JEWELLERY

Jewellery is small so easily transportable and you'll be able to keep some with you. That is why it is always worth checking the bodies of any zombies you have destroyed to see if they have anything of worth that you can take from their pockets. Although this may seem a little mercenary now, I can assure you it will be perfectly acceptable practice during a zombie outbreak and no one will think any less of you for robbing corpses (as long as you never let anyone catch you).

MORSE CODE

Dot dash dot dot dot dash dash dot dot dash dash dot dash dot dot dash dash dash dot dot dash dot cotton dash.

It is unlikely that many of you will be able to make much sense of what I have just written – even I can't make much sense of what I have just written.

Morse code is one of the most well-known codes in existence. Some of you may not understand the relevance of using code during the apocalypse – after all, the use of codes came about purely so that our wartime enemies could not decipher our messages to each other and during the apocalypse this will not be necessary as zombies don't particularly care that the eagle is going to fly at noon. On the contrary, it is wise to keep your Morse skills up to date as a more subtle means of communication. Zombies will react to the sound of human voices whether they are 'live' or transmitted across a radio. Therefore, if you have to make long-range communication, do it in the least vocal way possible: by using Morse code.

> **NOTE:** If you do not have an electronic device that will send Morse code then don't just say 'dot dot dash' into a radio. That is still using your voice and so will somewhat defeat the object of the exercise. You might as well just speak. Or stab yourself in the eye for even thinking of doing that in the first place.

MUSICAL INSTRUMENTS

Although someone once said something about music soothing the savage beast (could have been Shakespeare or maybe Barry Manilow), it is not a wise move to play any form of music at all during an apocalypse. The unfamiliar and melodic noises are liable to attract the undead but without the added bonus of the aforementioned soothing effects. No matter how practised you are in the art of playing a musical instrument, a zombie will still kill you (everyone's a critic). There is no need to throw your trombone straight into the bin though, as certain musical instruments may have a dual purpose and can be used as a weapon too.

Here we will look at how weapon techniques can be applied to various instruments. Take note that these are just suggestions that we have tested on members of the School of Survival; there may be other techniques you can come up with yourself that will work just as effectively. Feel free to freestyle and jam around a bit when using musical instruments as weapons.

Guitar

The effectiveness of a guitar depends on exactly which type of guitar you are planning to use. Acoustic guitars are generally hollow so will be highly ineffective as battering weapons as they will most likely fall apart on first impact. In contrast, the electric guitar is more solid and will withstand more hits and be capable of lasting until several of the undead have had their heads staved in.

The effectiveness of any guitar as a bludgeoning weapon is all dependent on the strength and length of the neck and heel/neck joint. Bear in mind that steel-stringed guitars have a stronger structural design in order to cope with the additional tension of the steel strings. But don't dismiss the acoustic guitar just yet. With slight adaptation the headstock can be whittled down in order to make the instrument into a pointy jabbing weapon or increasing the tension of the strings can turn it into a large bow to fire arrows, twigs, pencils and trumpets at the undead (this technique can also be applied to other smaller string instruments like violins).

Harp

Another stringed instrument. Once again this could be used as a bludgeoning weapon depending on its size and your strength, or as a 'bow' to catapult items long distances towards zombies. But it will ultimately be more effective, with the correct adjustments, as a zombie slicer.

Similar to an egg-slicing utensil, the strings of the harp are tough enough to swipe down through a zombie, thus cutting him into nice equal strips that you could lay on a ham sandwich if you were that way inclined.

Piano

Frankly, more practical as a barricade item as the weight and size of most pianos is enough to keep any door sealed. However, should you find that you are in need of a weapon, the piano can be broken down into segments and any of the large pieces used as bats (especially the lid from an upright or legs from a grand). Alternatively, those of you who are particularly fond of Laurel and Hardy films can use the piano to crush your enemy.

This is by no means a foolproof plan, as dropping large, irregularly shaped items on zombies does not necessarily mean that the brain will be destroyed. However, if you do retain part of the instrument prior to dropping it you will still have a batting weapon should the crushing technique not work.

Drums

There are over 45 different varieties of drums that are all constructed from different materials and components so it is difficult to generalise the use of this percussion instrument as a weapon. The majority of drums will be more effective as a defensive weapon than a damage-dealing one. Due to their size and shape, they are ideal for use as a shield to shove zombies away with.

The larger drums can also be used to restrain zombies by placing them over the zombie's head with force so the drum encircles its upper body thus rendering its arms useless. If you have a drum kit, it is the accessories that will be more useful as damage-dealing weapons. You can use the stands and sticks as stabbing weapons and the cymbals as large circular throwing discs (cymbals can be sharpened around the edges in order to be more effective).

Kazoo

There is a little-known technique to using a kazoo in times of crisis. Firstly, place the kazoo carefully in the centre of a table. Then, standing next to the table, place your hands on your hips. Now, repeatedly bash your face onto the table where the kazoo is sitting while repeating these words: 'Why do I own a kazoo? Why do I own a kazoo? Why do I own a kazoo?' Stop when you are unconscious or dead.

NAMES

'I have destroyed over 1000 of the undead. I have helped hundreds of survivors. I have fortified a city and helped to rebuild civilisation. I shall go down in history as a savior of mankind. For I am Cyril Leopold Catherine Twitterbumfrog III.'

Names are a funny old thing. We don't choose them, but we are stuck with them for our entire life and have to make the best of them. Very rarely do people make the effort to go and change their name – we all prefer to honour our parents' decision and stick with the moniker we've been blessed with.

The problem with names, though, is that they encourage us to form preconceptions about people before we've even met them. Take this example. You have heard of a team of survivors across town who have a large supply of weapons that they are willing to share with other survivors. All you have to do is head down to the old cinema complex, knock on the back fire exit and ask for their leader, Tarquin.

Now, it's quite possible that Tarquin is a strapping seven-foot ex-wrestler who is built like the proverbial brick toilet block, but that doesn't stop you imagining him sitting on a chaise draped in chiffon, listening to Noël Coward music playing on an old gramophone whilst sipping herbal tea – purely because he has the name Tarquin. Likewise, if the leader of this team was a woman named Shaz, most people would assume that this Shaz was unlikely to be a middle-aged woman who enjoyed knitting and the books of Agatha Christie, and was much more likely to have an affinity for tracksuits and White Lightning.

Names can also instil confidence in people. When it comes to crunch time, would you be more liable to vote for a man called Walter Shufflebottom to lead your team to glory on the battlefield against the undead or are you going to choose the chap who happens to be called Jack Power? With this in mind, you need to take a moment to assess your own name. Is it the kind of name that a leader would have? Is it the kind of name that will encourage men and women to follow you blindly into battle and trust your every decision? Is it a name that fits comfortably in front of the title 'Destroyer of Zombies'? If not, then as soon as the apocalypse begins you need to change it. (Don't bother changing it now. It will require you to do all kinds of pointless paperwork in order to get your bank accounts, bills, passports etc. in order. Time that could be better spent training. When the apocalypse comes you won't need to worry about the legal aspect of changing your name. As there won't be much law, you can just do it.)

The rule of thumb when picking a new name is that it needs to be short (this will make it quick and easy for your teammates to call out warnings to you); it needs to be memorable (so that people will be able to pass stories on about your prowess in battle); and it can't be too self-indulgent. Brad 'High Lord of the Urban Zones, Killer of a Thousand Brains and Destroyer of the Undead' may seem like a cool name now but when the apocalypse is finally over you'll find it a bugger when you have to start filling in job applications and writing cheques.

NAZI ZOMBIES

Let's be honest, no matter how much we desensitise ourselves to the walking dead, zombies are pretty terrifying really. They are almost unstoppable, attack en masse, feel no pain and could be a loved one or family member. At the very least, the thought of zombies is quite grim. However, despite this fact, there are still media executives sitting in shiny offices worldwide trying to find ways to make zombies more frightening.

'Hey,' *one of these executives might say at one of these meetings.* 'We've got a new movie coming out but we need to find a way to make these zombies a bit more terrifying than your average zombies.'

'How about making them into clowns?' *another executive might suggest.*

'Been done in *Zombieland* and *Left 4 Dead 2*,' *someone else would point out. Then they'd all look thoughtful for a moment until one of them bangs his fist on the desk.*

'Got it!'

'Hey! Bob's got an idea!'

'Well – and run with me on this – what's a really scary thing? You know, totally scarier than anything else you ever thought of?'

'Your wife first thing in the morning?' *They would then all guffaw and punch each other on the arm and make manly bonding sounds and nudge-wink faces. Once this has subsided the conversation would continue.*

'Go on, Bob, we're listening.'

'Nazis!'

'Nazis?'

'Zombie Nazis!'

'Wow, Bob – I think you may just have come up with the winner!'

'Let's put it to a focus group!'

'To hell with a focus group – let's do it!'

'Jeez, I feel good – let's go grab a steak and kill a hooker.'

'High five!'

This is obviously only an estimation of how the conversation may go and I, of course, have no definitive proof that media executives either eat steak or kill hookers – but my point is (and I do have one): is there any need to make zombies any scarier than they already are?

The fact is that Nazis weren't really very nice people – what with their xenophobia and silly moustaches and all. But if you turn one into a zombie they're not going to be any different than any other zombie – they are still going to want to kill and bite everyone they see. The only difference between a Nazi zombie and any other zombie is that the Nazi zombie would be wearing a Nazi uniform and there's not many people who walk the streets in Nazi uniforms in this day and age – because the general populace doesn't really like Nazis. So if you are a Nazi you're not actually going to advertise it by goose-stepping around in jodhpurs. The only folks who are likely to wear Nazi uniforms are people going to fancy dress parties or cast members from West End musicals. So instead of a terrifying army of Third Reich undead marching down the street towards you, you'll have Peter Kay or Gary Beach dressed in a sequined Hitler costume shambling along followed by a chorus of scantily clad German Beer Wenches. The point is that it's not really possible to make zombies any scarier than they already are – apart from if the Wheelers from *Return to Oz* became zombies – now that would be scary.

NEWS (TELEVISION)

'Welcome back to the most cutting edge news show on TV at the moment. It's the actual news, but edgier. I'm Bob Gold and later on we'll be talking to various experts about the apparent rise of the undead, but first this live report from Cynthia, who's on the spot at a local hospital. Cynthia?'

'Thanks, Bob! Despite the information we received from the most esteemed experts on the walking dead, here I am right at the edge of danger, ready to pick up multiple awards for my truthful, honest and daring news reporting tactics in a hospital that is currently being overrun by zombies. Look! There! A small child crying alone in a corner right where I placed him earlier. If that's not thought-provoking reporting I don't know what is. Back to you.'

'Thanks, Cynthia, we'll be back with you later. But first here's Graham with a large 3D graph.'

'Thanks, Bob, I also have a 3D pie chart too and a map of the world with big red blobs on it.'

'Insightful. What does it mean?'

'That we used up a fair whack of our yearly budget on pointless effects that have required us to lay off some of the cleaning staff.'

'But our viewers must see the truth in computer-generated graphics otherwise it won't make sense.'

'Absolutely – back to you Bob.'

'Thanks, Graham, now back to Cynthia at the local hospital to see how things are progressing.'

'Oh god… Oh god… They're dead… They're all dead and they're coming back to life! One of them's attacking Tom the Camera Guy! You've got to get me out of here! Oh no! Get them away from me! I'm going to die! Help! Bob!'

'Cynthia's going to die. You heard it here first and if that's not cutting edge I don't know what is. In a moment we'll be getting views on the escalating rise of the undead from the Minister for Bread, the outraged leader of a minority group and Sandi Toksvig. But first, the weather.'

'In 3D, Bob!'

'Yes, in 3D.'

NOISE

To avoid attracting the undead to your location you should make as little noise as possible – of course, we all know that.

You will also have to rely more heavily on your senses during the apocalypse. For instance, being able to recognise particular noises will be a skill that will be invaluable to you when attempting to survive.

A zombie's guttural moan is quite distinctive. It is not known whether the noise is made on purpose or whether it is merely caused by the air passing through its slowly rotting vocal chords. But a zombie does make this noise and if you hear it, you will know that a member of the undead is nearby.

You may think it will be easy to recognise this particular sound and you're probably right. When you're in the middle of a deserted city and you hear a moan, you can pretty much guarantee that it will be a zombie heading in your direction... Or will it? Could it be another wounded survivor moaning in pain? You wouldn't want to call off a scavenging mission to collect food that could save your team from death just because you heard an old man groaning about a cramped leg.

It is true that the groans of the undead will sound very similar to the groans of a human being – but if we listen very carefully to the two you will notice a distinct difference.

Tests have been carried out on how the vocal chords operate and once they begin to degrade they operate in a different way. Now, I'm not exactly sure how this is going to translate to the written word, but believe me, when you listen to the examples it's quite obvious to hear the tonal differences between healthy vocal chords operating and dead ones.

A healthy human moaning in pain would sound like this: Ooooooh. Whereas a zombie would sound like this: Oooooourgh.

Let's listen to that again.

Healthy: *Ooooooooh.*
Zombie: *Oooooourgh.*

Are you getting this?

Healthy: *Ooooooooh.*
Zombie: *Oooooourgh.*

...this isn't really working, is it? Perhaps if you tried to emulate the sounds as they're written... No...no, that's no good. Look, I'm just going to have to finish this segment here. What started off as quite a serious point has just been turned into a complete mockery. Maybe if you did your own tests on degraded vocal chords that might help. Just go down the hospital and see if you can borrow a cadaver. Hey! Look! I'm just trying to salvage my point here! Don't look at me like that! Fine, we'll just skip it – zombie noises aren't that important anyway.

NUDITY

I think we've already established that nudity is not the best way to present yourself during a zombie apocalypse. However, the zombies you encounter in an apocalypse may well be naked and you need to be prepared for that fact.

When the zombie infection first takes hold, and nobody

realises what is going on, most people who are feeling ill will go to bed. People tend to wear very little, if anything, in bed, especially if they are running a fever. There is a good chance then, that many people will die naked and thus they will be reanimated naked – and I can assure you that these undead will have absolutely no shame when it comes to flaunting themselves for all to see. They won't be bothered about slipping on a pair of slacks and a cardie before leaving the house. Their state of undress will not deter them from coming at you and you don't want to let this fact be your downfall.

Nudity can be somewhat distracting (especially if it's someone you know) so you need to prepare yourself. Not only will the undead be attempting to take a chunk out of you, but their naughty bits will be flapping in the breeze too. If your attacker is naked then just follow some simple rules:

1) Remember, whether you have nudity to contend with or not, your prime objective is still the same – to destroy the brain. Do not be put off from that task by embarrassment, awkwardness or penis envy.

2) Keep eye contact with your attacker; this will stop you becoming distracted by any endowments that the zombie could have.

3) Do not try and cop a feel. There will be time enough for that later – once you have destroyed the brain and your attacker is down.

NUKED

Picture the scene. You have managed to find yourself a secure safe house and you've got all the weapons and supplies you need to last for at least six months. You have managed to get all your loved ones into your sanctuary with you and there is an attractive person to hand to enable effective repopulation when the whole affair is over.

Then the authorities go and drop a nuclear bomb on you. From reading this training manual, you will have come to the conclusion that zombies will not be your only problem. You should bear in mind that some brainless bureaucrat may take it upon themselves to start blowing up urban areas in order to attempt to control the spread of the undead. Even if you paint a sign on your roof trumpeting your presence and the fact that you are still alive, they will just look upon you as collateral damage – one person who must be sacrificed in order to save the many. This is why, at your earliest and safest opportunity, you should attempt to vacate urban areas and get out into the country. There you can watch the beautiful mushroom clouds blossom all around you and die a much more slow and painful death due to radiation poisoning.

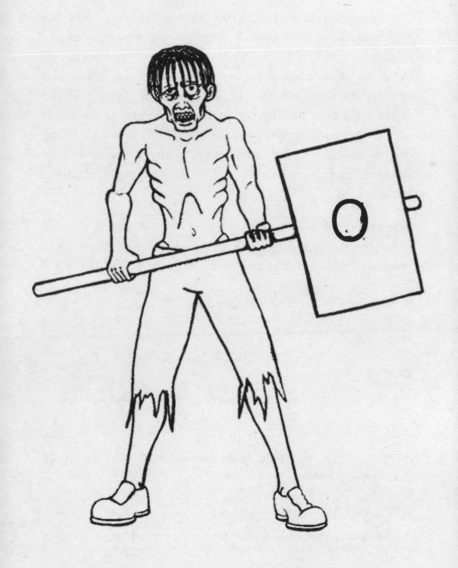

...OF THE DEAD

The definitive guide to most things apocalypse-related lies within the films of George A. Romero. The man who single-handedly reinvented the genre for modern audiences, he leaves no stone unturned when investigating the cause and effect of the living dead as they rise from their graves, whilst at the same time passing comment on the state of the world we live in today. Anyone who is truly serious about surviving the apocalypse should watch the complete collection of Romero movies and ingest every morsel of information within them.

Survival of the Dead

What you doing, George? You trying to make my whole point moot? I just don't want to talk about it...

Night of the Living Dead

A group of people hide from bloodthirsty zombies in a farmhouse.

Dawn of the Dead

A group of people hide from bloodthirsty zombies in a mall.

Day of the Dead

A group of people hide from bloodthirsty zombies in an underground bunker.

Land of the Dead

A group of people hide from bloodthirsty zombies in a walled city.

Diary of the Dead

A group of people decide not to hide from bloodthirsty zombies but film them instead. Then they realise that that was a silly idea and hide in a mansion.

Dairy of the Dead

A group of people hide from bloodthirsty zombies in a cheese factory and eat lots of cheese… Or that may have been a dream I had…

OBSTACLE COURSE

This is probably the worst place to be when being chased by a zombie. If you happen to find yourself on an army base or the set of *The Krypton Factor* when the zombies attack, then ensure that you don't get trapped on the obstacle course. You will have to run through tyres and swing across muddy puddles and walk across thin planks of wood, and if you do fall off, you'll have to go back and start again. All of this will also be more tiring than running across flat terrain.

If you are unable to steer clear of the obstacle course then just hope that it has one of those really tall walls with a knotted rope for you to climb over with. The zombies won't be able to scale it effectively as they can't climb. There is the faint possibility that they may realise they can walk around it…but that's cheating so here's hoping they'll stick to the rules.

ORIGAMI

Ever had a paper cut? Lethal, aren't they? Imagine building an axe or a sword out of paper! That would be doubly lethal…or just plain stupid. Either way, it passes the time.

OTHER SURVIVORS

In an apocalypse we won't just have the zombies to worry about. Oh, no siree, Bob. And I'm not just talking about those troublesome authorities or even those loony bins who crack under the pressure. There are also the other – quite 'sane' – survivors to worry about, who may end up being your downfall. And we wouldn't want you being popped off by just another plain, old human being. Here's a few of the rotters that you'll need to look out for:

The cultist
Whenever there's a disaster there's always a religious leader around to take advantage of people's fear and confusion. Even

if all the religious leaders have been torn asunder by their zombified choirboys, there will always be someone left who believes that they have been chosen to lead the new dawn and become the divine one. Their reasoning is that God has spared them and you do wonder if maybe God did have some kind of plan for this kind of person because it's a mystery how they would have survived thus far without any divine intervention.

The reason you need to be wary around these people is that they have usually amassed a group of followers who will do anything their leader commands (under the misapprehension that it is the word of the Lord) and if the leader sees you as a threat he may set his legions on you to retain his control or force you to join them and wear a silly mask and a yellow anorak. Death or anorak? Difficult choice.

The hoarder

People who were organised when the apocalypse first began. They have managed to secure a great deal of highly sought-after supplies and will part with them for no amount of begging or bartering. Usually they will have moved the supplies to one main, extremely secure holding area, but in some cases they may have 'staked a claim' on other buildings, such as warehouses or large stores, where it is easier to leave the items in situ than move them. In this case you will be classed as a looter if you are found raiding these buildings and may be punished or killed. It is best to pay heed to any signs of territory and move on. There will be enough supplies to be found in the next town or village.

The highwayman

The ones who rob you. I think that it's pretty self-explanatory what the problem with these guys is. Yes, that's right. They come in and reorganise your kitchen so you can't find anything. No!

They rob you! Steal your stuff! All your stuff! Including, but not limited to, your stuff! All of it! Kill them.

The Soloist

That lone wolf who sits brooding in a darkened room smoking an endless supply of cigarettes and toting his bloodied hunting knife. He wears nothing but his ripped jeans (mid-blue) and a sleeveless combat jacket to show off his rippling tattooed arms. The stubble on his face is indiscernible from the dirt and dried blood. He has usually decided to go it alone because his entire family was annihilated within the first few minutes of the outbreak and he has vowed to destroy every last zombie.

He is reckless and doesn't take orders, and he wouldn't think twice about killing you should you distract him from his mission. Stay away from him. He may be strong and deadly but he's also extremely depressing to be around and will ruin any party you decide to have.

FEMALE SOLOISTS

The soloist can just as easily be a woman who will take on exactly the same appearance – just replace the 'stubble on his face' with 'stubble on her legs'.

The master

'I'm king of the world!' No – he's neither Jack Dawson nor James Cameron accepting an Oscar. This survivor thinks that due to the death of all others he is rightful ruler of the city/country/world/universe (depending on what this person believes they rule could topple them over into our insanity segment). It is quite likely that they are also 'hoarders' with a large store of supplies that they won't share.

The difference between being a master as well as a hoarder is that they are attempting to instil their own form of law onto the land that doesn't just bear on looting. They may wish to take several wives. They could charge taxes for travelling across their land. They could enslave you. Like 'cultists', they will have a large group of followers who will do their bidding.

These followers are not as stable as a religious following, though, as they will only stay loyal to those in power. Either way, you really need to avoid these guys, as the last thing you need to become involved in is a turf war whilst the undead are still lumbering around. The master also has a tendency for complacency as he sits resting on his laurels, which will ultimately lead to him being bitten.

The Shoot-firsters

As you go sauntering down a deserted street minding your own business, taking in the fresh air and looking for food and weapons, the last thing you expect is for a bullet to embed itself between your eyes. There are survivors out there, though, who understandably will shoot or kill anything that moves.

When travelling the streets you must react as if you are in a war zone. Don't just keep your eyes open at ground level for the undead. You also need to look above for signs of life just to make sure that you don't get shot or get a piano dropped on you, or a sofa, or a filing cabinet, or a bed or a... Actually, the list is endless really so I'm going to stop there. Suffice to say that other survivors may drop things off buildings hoping to hit you thinking that you're a zombie. Actually, it's unlikely they'd drop a tulip on you so maybe the list isn't endless, after all. You get the point though.

The Meek

It is said that the meek shall inherit the Earth. Not bleedin' likely, matey. Not if they continue to weep and wail and wander aimlessly about putting themselves directly in harm's way so that they constantly have to be rescued. The meek will just get killed is what'll happen, and then they'll turn into zombies and then they'll take over the world... Oh! I see what it's getting at now!

OUIJA BOARD

Here's an interesting theory. Once a zombie reanimates we all know that there is no longer anything human about them. The human part of them has died and what is left is a feral monster that is driven by an infection and the lust for living flesh. The fact that death occurs *prior* to reanimation means that technically the person's soul should have gone somewhere. So for those who believe in ghosts and the spirit world, it should mean that we will still be able to communicate with our loved ones after death because it is only their body that is still active and not their soul.

It is also a well-documented fact for those who believe in ghostly goings-on and watch *Most Haunted* on a regular basis that spirits are more likely to manifest themselves if they have suffered a violent and untimely death – and not surprisingly, there will be a lot of that kind of thing going on during a zombie apocalypse.

So, does that mean that there will be restless spirits roaming our zombified cities as well as the undead? If so, are they likely to try and help us? And if they can, how do we contact them? The Ouija board, of course.

In the absence of having a trained medium or Yvette Fielding on your team of survivors (and you don't want Yvette on your team. She's really jumpy and even after years of presenting a programme about ghosts, she squeals at the slightest noise). Your next best bet is to try and make yourself a Ouija board. This can be done by only using the 'Yes' and 'No' answers or you can include every single letter of the alphabet to allow the spirit to give more detailed answers. You then overturn a glass, everyone involved puts their finger on it and you ask the question 'Is anybody there?' Then Bob's your uncle, the spirits contact you. (It may, actually, not be as easy as all that and may take a bit of tension-building first and the occasional flash of lightning or the lights flickering on and off. Anyway, at some point the spirits may or may not get in touch.)

Once you have made contact, you can use the spirits to let you know things like where the best supplies are, if you are going to survive and where One-Eyed Willy's secret treasure is buried. And I'm sure they'd be more than willing to help seeing as some evil force has taken over their body and is currently dragging its heels about outside looking for people to rip apart.

If the dead don't happen to get in touch on this particular occasion then all might not be lost. Use your own finger to point the glass to members of the team you don't particularly like and send them out on suicide missions while pretending to be possessed by the spirit of Great Uncle Mortimer. The only thing you have to remember with this is that when they get to the afterlife they will probably discover from Great Uncle Mortimer that he wasn't the one who sent the message and that it was actually you and then they could come back and possess you and force you to make a vase out of clay on a pottery wheel or some other such heinous task. Of course, all of this is irrelevant if you don't really believe in this kind of thing, because if you don't believe in it then it can't really exist, can it?

Please note that the last question was rhetorical and the theory of not believing in something meaning it doesn't exist doesn't work. If that were the case I wouldn't believe in the zombie apocalypse, meaning that it wouldn't exist. I wouldn't believe in racial intolerance, meaning that wouldn't exist, and I also wouldn't believe in the combined hits of Sophie Ellis Bextor, Gina G and the Cheeky Girls because I *really* wish they didn't exist.

OUTBOARD MOTOR

Useful for propelling a boat (see **Boats**) but I would also imagine it would be quite fun to start one up and then stick it in a zombie's face thus blending its head. Or that may just be taking the whole art of zombie killing just a little too far. With that in mind, though, if you don't have a blender to make your morning smoothie, you could always use a bucket and an outboard motor. Or a power drill in a jug.

OUTSIDE

Try and go there as little as possible.

PANIC ZONES

This is one of the things that will get the most people killed in an initial outbreak and will cause the greatest spread of the undead across the globe, yet it would be so easy to stop if people just used their noggin for a moment. People won't though. You know that and I know that. The general public is essentially stupid when it comes to times of crisis and will flood to their own reanimated death in these quarters of doom known as Panic Zones.

So what exactly are panic zones? There are several classifications that I will look into now. Avoid them at all costs.

BEFORE:

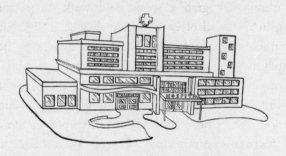

AFTER:

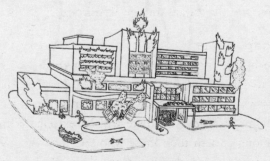

The Outbreak Zone

Hospitals are the prime example of this type of panic zone. At the first signs of an outbreak, those who are infected will rush themselves or their loved ones to hospital. The hospital staff won't know what's going on and neither will the patients. Then the patients will die, and in due course start to reanimate. The many sick and vulnerable people in the hospital will find it difficult to fight back so you will have a huge number of people all reanimated very quickly. And as more people arrive with no idea of what's going on inside, the circle of death will continue.

The Answer Zone

When a crisis begins everyone thinks they're a hero, but that doesn't mean they grab a shovel and walk down the street smashing in the head of every corpse they see. No, that would be the sensible thing to do. They think that the way to be a hero is to march down to the nearest authority (police station, council office, army barracks) and demand answers. They'll be shouting and bawling at those in power who could be doing a much more effective job if they didn't have half the city's population camped on their doorstep screaming and shouting about the ignominy of the situation rather than doing anything proactive about it. So there you have it. Crowds of people all in one place. All it takes is one zombie and the rest, as they say, is history.

The Escape Zone

Once the horror of the situation sinks in there will be a mad clamour to get out of infected areas. Airports, train stations, and ports will all be flooded with people wanting to get away as quickly as possible. And there will be extremely impractical people amongst them too. Those who see fit to take with them all their worldly goods including their clothes, television, washing machine and Ikea flat-pack house. During a zombie apocalypse so many people crammed into one place is once again setting the scene for a mass infection. The real stupidity of the situation is that the transport system in the UK is never very reliable at the best of times, so why would anyone assume it would be running at perfect capacity when there's a crisis on?

MAIN ROADS

These are also classed as panic zones as those travelling by car will also clog up the primary exit routes from a city. Although not as dangerous as crowded areas, the long lines of cars filled with the living will be like a trail of breadcrumbs leading the undead to more victims – but ultimately clearing urban areas of larger hordes.

The Supply Zone

We need cheese! This may be the cry of the masses as they hear of a possible crisis. And not just cheese, but any form of dairy products, food, weapons, stationery, fuel and all manner of useless stuff. There is nothing the general public like more than panic-buying when a 'situation' occurs. Every year over the Christmas period shops are bled dry of every possible form of foodstuff because they are closed for a few days over the New Year period. So imagine the shopathon that will occur if the undead rise. It will be like *Supermarket Sweep* with bludgeoning weapons instead of Dale Winton (or Dale Winton being used as a bludgeoning weapon!). And although these panic zones will be filled with aggressive folks all trying to purchase what they believe is necessary, that aggression will make them blind to their own safety – these areas will be easy pickings for a zombie intent on doing his own taste-testing.

The God Help Me Zone

When all else fails, turn to God. If the authorities and medical science can't supply the answers then turn to the deity who is to blame and has the power to save us from everything. Even the non-religious find time for prayer when all else has failed, and houses of worship for all denominations will become overcrowded with over-emotional people seeking redemption and hope. The consolation is that in these areas religious buildings have always been built as sanctuaries and will likely be able to keep the undead out for a reasonable period of time – if the people within are sensible enough to keep the doors closed. However, it only takes one good Samaritan to let a victim who has been bitten into the building and the whole situation will go tits up (although you wouldn't refer to the situation in that manner in a place of religious worship as *tits* is somewhat of an ungodly word).

Those who will have resorted to taking shelter in a church will also be at the stage of complete panic or complete resignation and are liable to be wailing and moaning. The noise is likely to attract the attention of the walking dead who, although they may not be able to get into the building, will make it pretty damn difficult for anyone to get out. Places of worship are not well known for stocking large quantities of food (unless wine and very thin slices of bread are favourites of yours) so eventually those inside will either starve to death or die attempting to get supplies.

In essence, a panic zone is a place that is overrun with the unprepared general public when the apocalypse is in its early stages. Anywhere that stupid people are liable to head should be avoided at all costs. As we all know, the first thing you should do is get inside and lie low (preferably on a higher floor in a secure building, but sometimes beggars can't be choosers). Panic zones are not to be confused with 'infection hotspots'. These are areas that are already crowded prior to anyone having knowledge of the apocalypse (e.g. music concerts, sporting events, lecture halls and theatres). Some of these could make excellent safe houses when abandoned but if they are full during an outbreak, can become infection hotspots. And what's a hotspot not? I think we all know the answer to that one.

PHOBIAS

Necrophobia is the fear of death and dead things; hence, if you are afraid of zombies you are a sufferer of necrophobia. Obviously you're not afraid of the dead, otherwise you wouldn't have bought this book – but you must be afraid of dying or you wouldn't have bought this book. Technically, that would make you a half a necrophobic – afraid of death but not dead things – a rophobic if you will. But we'll soon cure that, as you're not going to die because you bought this book.

Phobias are a serious problem for a lot of people and when we talk about a phobia we don't just mean you saw a tiny spider and squeaked like a girl and jumped on a chair. A true phobic is paralysed by their particular fear and goes cold at the very thought of it, and sweats and shakes beyond control. These are the kind of phobias that need sorting out before the apocalypse begins as debilitating fear will almost certainly affect how you react in certain situations.

Those with acrophobia will not be able to secure themselves in buildings with any height. Pathophobics, bacteriophobics, verminophobics and mysophobics will be completely incapable of coping with cities in ruin and the lack of hygiene and order. Hemophobics will find it difficult to do any killing and dendrophobics won't be able to take cover in a forest. If you believe for one second that your irrational phobia will hinder your survival in any way then you must become cured immediately. No! Not later! Now! Put the book down and deal with your mental problems before it gets you killed. This isn't something that can take weeks in therapy either. What if the apocalypse were to start tomorrow? You need to be ready! So, if you are afraid of spiders you need to get down to your local pet shop and buy a tarantula. Go on! And don't come back until you've got one…

Got one? Good, we're going to deal with this problem immediately. There are no small steps to be taken. I want you to take that tarantula out of its carrier bag and put it in your mouth. There we go! You're cured! Hello? Hello! Oh! You can take it out now. See, that wasn't too hard, was it? You are now cured of your fear even though you may very well be scarred for life. The fact that you overcame a silly little phobia speaks volumes for your strength of character. At least yours was a serious phobia – some spiders can actually be dangerous! Think of the poor sods who suffer from alektorophobia (chickens) porphyrophobia (the colour purple – the actual colour of purple, not the film) and coulrophobia (fear of clowns). And don't even get me started on genophobics – who knows what I would have made them put in their mouths.

PHYSICAL AILMENTS

Any kind of physical ailment is liable to slow down your progress in surviving a zombie apocalypse, be it a minor case of indigestion or a complete lack of legs. Either way you're just going to have to suck it up and get on with it if you want any hope of surviving at all. Anyone can survive a zombie apocalypse. It's not about your physical capabilities, it's about your knowledge and how you use it. And the knowledge that physical ailments pass on to the undead is good to know.

Death is not a magical cure for all physical ailments, and if you have kidney stones when alive, unless something is done about them, they will remain when you are dead – and hence when you are undead too. But although kidney stones might be painful to a living human, they are not going to affect a zombie who is impervious to pain, so that piece of knowledge isn't particularly important.

Here's the important bit: if a person is blind in life, if they are bitten and become a zombie they'll be blind too. If a person is deaf in life, once reanimated as a zombie they will still be deaf. If a person is paralysed then it figures that when transformed the zombie will also be paralysed. So, should you know the person who has been transformed and know of any physical ailments they possessed in life, this may give you the edge you need to defeat them.

This is also true of age. Becoming a member of the undead does not suddenly imbue you with superhuman strength. A child zombie will still only have the strength they had when a child and, likewise, an older zombie may suffer from advanced joint problems if they've not been taking their cod liver oil regularly.

Being aware of this will enable you to make informed decisions regarding the safest place to secure yourself and scavenge, as you must also know your own capabilities. (See **Demographics**). If you are not the kind of person who could survive a fight with a gang of football hooligans, don't go to a football stadium. Likewise, if you really don't feel you have the physical strength to take on a horde of old ladies, steer clear of bingo halls.

PIXIES

Don't exist.

PLANE

OK, before anyone says anything, I realise that technically this should have fallen under the entry 'Aeroplane' and that by placing it here people may be confused and think I was going to talk about the plane that is actually a tool for shaving wood, or indeed the River Plane in Germany.

Unfortunately, due to the space constraints under A, there wasn't any room to fit in a segment to talk about aeroplanes. But there are some important points to be made so I am left with no choice but to write about it here under the abbreviated title of '**Plane**'.

So my apologies to those who believed they would learn some interesting weapon techniques for the humble plane (tool, not the river) or to those who were hoping to find suitable areas of sanctuary along the side of the Plane (river, not the tool) because this segment is going to be entirely dedicated to the kind of plane that flies in the air – or known by its full name – the aeroplane… Well, that's what the segment would have been about if I hadn't run out of space again.

POPULATION (DENSITY)

Don't go to Dhaka in the event of a zombie apocalypse. If you are in Dhaka in the event of a zombie apocalypse, get out immediately. In fact, if you are in Dhaka at this very moment then book your tickets out of there now. As Dhaka has a population of almost seven million it may be quite difficult to get a bus once the apocalypse has begun and even if you do you'll probably have to stand, which can cause cramping during long-haul journeys.

Dhaka, in Bangladesh, is the most densely populated city in the world, closely followed by Manila, in the Philippines. Of course, when attempting to avoid being bitten by the undead the fewer people who are around to be transformed into zombies the better. It is a common misconception that we should look at the population when assessing the safety of an area during a zombie apocalypse. If this were the case, with a population of 6,733,164,238 we should consider getting off planet Earth and maybe moving somewhere with a few less people, like the sun. No! Population density is where it's at when trying to keep safe (not to be confused with population dentistry, which is how we keep the world's teeth safe).

We all know that the People's Republic of China is the most populated country in the world, with a whopping 1,331,650,000 citizens (and if you didn't know that you should visit Wikipedia on a more regular basis). However, because of its sheer size this population is spread over a vast area (3,705,407 square miles) making it number 75 on the Most Densely Populated Countries in the World chart (similar to the music chart but with less music and with more people counting and no platinum disc if you do really well).

This information means that, country-wise, the People's Republic of China is actually a safer place to be in a zombie apocalypse than the United Kingdom (which comes in at number 52 with a population of almost 70 million over 93,800 square miles) or Guernsey and Jersey, which come in at 12th and 13th respectively (and that's not including the cows).

It is worth noting though that whilst it is quite easy to come by statistics of the most densely populated areas – statistics on areas with the lowest population density are harder to come by. But simply using the word 'city' to describe an area should conjure up images of a lot of people milling about. To ensure that you are heading towards an area with low population density, look for words on a map like 'village', 'hamlet' or 'swamp'.

POSITIVE THINKING

OK, so the majority of inspirational self-help gabble can be disregarded as complete bunkum and is best saved for scrawling across pictures of cute animals on the wall of mundane accountancy offices in middle-England. (Oh look! There's a kitten hanging from a tree and underneath it says 'Hang in there!' Isn't that cute? Although maybe someone should save the kitten before it falls and breaks its spine rather than taking a picture of it.)

There is something to be said for the power of positive thought though. Those with the ability to hold a cheery disposition and exude a proactive vibe will have a 70% higher chance of surviving the apocalypse, and that's the same percentage as women who say they've had sexual health problems according to a survey conducted by Harris Interactive in 2010, so that must mean something.

You may think it will be difficult to stay positive when the world around you is turning to hell in a hand basket. But, as the old saying goes, every cloud has a silver lining; all you have to do is look for it. Here are a few examples of how to keep positive during the zombie apocalypse:

Situation: The undead have risen.
Positive thinking: You will no longer have to worry about paying utility bills or clearing the balance of your credit cards.

Situation: A loved one has been transformed into a zombie.
Positive thinking: One less present to buy at Christmas.

Situation: Your safe house is surrounded by zombies and you've run out of food.
Positive thinking: Think of the weight you'll lose, and whilst you can't go out, you can get on with the odd jobs you've been putting off, like regrouting the tiles in the bathroom.

Situation: Zombies have invaded your safe house and you have taken refuge in a very small cupboard.

Positive thinking: Now you've got some alone time you can start reassessing your life and maybe even make a start on that novel you've been thinking about. Plan out a synopsis and some character outlines by scratching notes onto the inside of the cupboard door with your fingernails.

Situation: You've been bitten and are going to die and turn into a zombie.

Positive thinking: Actually there's nothing really positive about this for you. The only good thing about it is that the other members of your team won't have to put up with your positive attitude anymore which was frankly quite annoying.

QUARANTINE

I think I may have already mentioned that there is no cure for the zombie virus. That means that allowing anyone near you who may even vaguely, possibly have been bitten by something that may or may not have been a zombie should be killed immediately. By killing their brain. In a fashion that kills them.

This means that you should disregard the idea of quarantine. It is a pointless endeavour with so many flaws. Even top-secret scientists with top-secret labs and top-secret quarantine chambers that are made from fully reinforced glass are not safe when operating quarantine procedures. Do you people not watch the movies?

Let's look at an example. Let's say that your brother may have been bitten. You're not sure so you don't want to kill his brain without positive proof. The only positive proof you're going to get is when he finally transforms. Now, you could argue that all you would do is wait for him to get ill before taking the decision to dispose of him, but I'm not buying that. You'd only make the excuse that it could be a cold, or shock, or heroin addiction that was making him turn pale and shake. You'd wait until he actually died before contemplating any brain killing. But here are some points to take into consideration:

Do you have a glass room where you can contain him and also watch him continually at the same time? No? So you're planning to just tie him to a chair and lock him in a room without 24-hour surveillance leaving the possibility that he may die and reanimate and escape and kill you all before anyone notices. Oh! That wasn't the plan? You were going to tie him to a chair in a locked room and rotate surveillance on him by actually being in the room. As in, be in the room with someone who isn't a zombie and thus cut down on the people guarding the safe house against actual real zombies? OK, no, sorry, I wasn't being condescending, that sounds really sensible.

So when he dies, you're going to go right up to his body and check his pulse just to make sure he's dead even though you don't know how quickly he's going to reanimate. You're not? So how do you know he's dead? He may just be sleeping and then if you shoot him you could be killing someone who wasn't dead. Oh! You're going to wait until he reanimates! Even though he may immediately come round and attack you and will be moving erratically making it more difficult to guarantee a head shot. Plus, if you don't have a long-range weapon you're going to have to get up close and put yourself at risk of being bitten. And then you may sustain a wound that may or may not be a bite and the whole damn quarantine rigmarole will have to begin all over again. Do you really want me to adopt this sarcastic tone again and explain for a second time everything that could possibly go wrong with using quarantines?

ESCAPEES

Even if you do have a reinforced glass quarantine chamber in a secret lab, stop using it now. The zombie will always escape. I don't care how safe you think it is. It will escape. Always! Listen to me! Right! Fine! Kill yourself. See if I care.

QUESTIONNAIRE

We're over halfway through the book now, so let's see what you've learnt so far in this short but revealing questionnaire. Answer as truthfully and honestly as possible and don't cheat by looking at the answers first.

Question One

You are sitting outside having a skinny latte and chocolate muffin at an Italian style patisserie in the middle of an urban area when you receive word that the dead have started to rise. What is the first thing you do?

a) Finish your coffee and muffin. You haven't paid £7.30 for the privilege of sitting in this trumped up café for your beverage and very small snack to go to waste.

b) Leap onto the table screaming 'The dead are coming! The dead are coming!' whilst rubbing your muffin into your hair and pouring your latte down the front of your trousers.

c) Hide.

Question Two

You have overcome the first few days of the apocalypse and must now find a place to set up a permanent safe house. Which of the following options is the most sensible?

a) I'll be able to think more clearly when I've finished my latte and muffin.

b) The top floor of a high-rise block of flats.

c) A teepee.

Question Three

A zombie has spotted you and has started to shamble towards you intent on taking a large bite out of your face and turning you into one of its undead friends. What do you do?

a) For God's sake! Can I not finish this damn muffin in peace?

b) Run away and hide. You can outrun a zombie while close combat could result in you being bitten.

c) A teepee.

Question Four

You have secured yourself in a safe house when a small, dirty and bloodied child comes knocking and crying and asking you for help. What should you do?

a) Allow the child safe passage through your kingdom on the condition they answer three riddles correctly.

b) Turn the child away. You cannot afford to put yourself at risk.

c) Eat the child.

Question Five

You have been bitten by a zombie. What should you do?

a) Bite the bugger back! That'll teach him!

b) Immediately kill yourself by destroying your own brain so you do not rise again.

c) Become enraged and disorientated and climb to the top of the empire state building whilst holding onto Faye Wray as biplanes attempt to shoot you down.

Question Six

Is there a cure for the zombie virus?

a) Yes.

b) No.

c) A teepee.

What this questionnaire tells you:

Mostly As

You are a strong-minded individual who doesn't mind using their sexual power to get what they want. But being a little bit flirty and a little bit dirty isn't always the best way to gain friends. Try using a gentler, more understanding approach and you may be pleasantly surprised at the reaction you get.

Mostly Bs

Your perfect partner is someone who will love you for who you are. They will be able to give as good as they get whilst still getting as good as they give. They will stroke your hair whilst reading the sonnets of Shakespeare to you on cold winter nights. They will love Italian food, French cinema and Spanish wine. They will be honest and loving and not be too rash with financial decisions. They will be ginger.

Mostly Cs

A teepee.

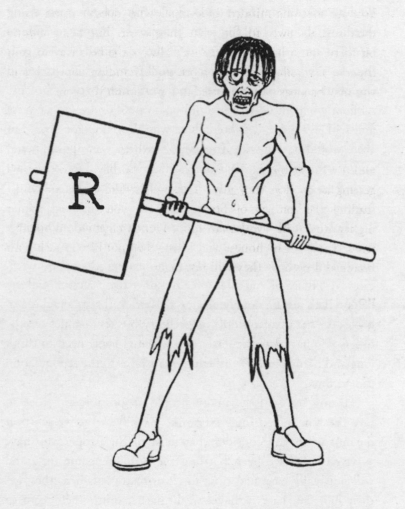

REPOPULATION

It's all well and good surviving a great disaster, but it doesn't do humankind much good if you've not planned on doing anything about rebuilding the completely decimated human race. I'm sorry to say, that as one of the few survivors, it is your duty to repopulate the planet as quickly as possible to aid in the continuance of mankind (and womankind too – because without womankind there would be no mankind and vice versa and with no Judge Reinhold there would be no *Vice Versa*, but there would be *Big* with Tom Hanks which was slightly better and not forgetting *Freaky Friday* which was like *Vice Versa* only with females. See, we couldn't have one without the other… I digress).

Those who need any help in the art of repopulation probably need to reevaluate their lives a little bit. Possibly starting by thinking less about the undead and more about the opposite sex. However, those of you who already know the basics of 'making babies' (let's just be doubly clear at this point that the making of babies doesn't involve storks, gooseberry bushes or toilet seats… unless you have a particularly kinky sexual bent) need to think long and hard before committing themselves to the repopulation programme.

Having sex with as many people as possible in order to save the human race may seem like a really attractive prospect but not when you consider that most of the people who have survived will have been battling the dead for some time and will not really have had time to clean or iron their clothes, get their hair cut, have a shave, wash, bathe, brush their teeth or spend a few sessions on the sunbed. Most survivors are liable to smell just a little bit too. Women who opt to help rebuild the population of the earth will most likely spend the rest of their adult life pregnant and men will have to continually have sex – and although I'm sure this task won't have put off many men be aware that you will be unable to build a relationship with either your offspring or the mother of your child (or children).

If the zombies have *not* yet been fully defeated you will be bringing a new generation into the world who will continue to fight on behalf of the human race. And if the zombies *have* been defeated, the children who are born will grow up in a world that needs a hell of a lot of cleaning up doing. Whichever way you look at it, any child born into a world after the zombies have risen is going to have to make a really hard slog of it. But bear in mind that by opting to repopulate and bring them into the world in the first place you'll have done most of the hard work. The people you sleep with won't have washed for god's sake!

RICOCHET

If you shoot this gun correctly then the bullet will bounce off that beam up above us and then hit that dustbin. It will then ricochet into the pile of bricks on the floor and then ricochet back against that plank of wood that is leaning against the wall. It will traverse those crates and bounce off the opposing wall into that fridge, onto the ceiling and then straight down onto that zombie's head, thus killing him!

Or you could wait until the zombie gets a bit closer and hit it with a stick.

ROBOTS

Technology has come a long way since the early sixteenth century. I would not be typing this on a computer for one thing; I'd be plucking a chicken or a golden eagle and dipping it's feathers in a pot of ink – or maybe even scraping the entries into blocks of stone with a flint which would mean this book would be really heavy and would probably cost a fortune to ship from Amazon – but I seem to be digressing…

These days we rely on machines to do a lot of our work for us, especially the more dangerous work. There are bomb disposal robots, search and rescue robots, robots to split atoms, robots to carry out surgical procedures, robots to visit distant planets and robots that can operate WMD. Of course, although no one has fully perfected artificial intelligence yet, putting these robots in dangerous situations with scant regard for their safety and also giving them control of our weapons systems will ultimately lead to a Skynet situation where the robots will take over the world and we will have to lead a revolt against them and battle just to stay alive, which is a whole other book on survival techniques (available soon: *Dr Dale's Dictionary of How to Survive a Skynet Situation Where the Robots Take Over the World and We Have to Lead a Revolt Against Them and Battle Just to Stay Alive*). In the meantime, if the zombie apocalypse occurs first (which is more likely), much like any other mechanical object listed in this dictionary, if you have the means to keep it working and it doesn't take up too much time in maintenance, then by all means use the robot to go out and fetch supplies or battle the undead or protect your safe house or whatever else you can think of that it could do to help you survive.

Note: If you own a robodog then these are pretty useless in aiding in survival. Just because they can sense where a wall is doesn't make them that useful to you. Instead of using the robodog to find a wall, why not use…say…your eyes! Yes, yes, robodog makes cute barking noises (that will no doubt draw the undead to your location) and does a back flip that is mildly amusing. However, to gain the most use from a robodog, pick it up and smash it over a zombie's head repeatedly until neither the dog – or the zombie – works anymore. This is referred to as killing two birds with one stone.

ROLE PLAYING

Seen by many as a pastime for geeks who sit around a table with 97-sided dice, pointy wizard hats and silly, unpronounceable alter egos (in Elven), role playing in its many forms is not something that should be mocked. Yes, you may very well have spent your formative years downing kegs of beer, dressing in togas and engaging in potentially homoerotic hazing activities in a dorm room with twelve football players and a goat (which was no doubt fun at the time) but what is going to be better value in preparing you for the apocalypse? Partying hard or RPGs?

When soldiers prepare for battle they do so by going through training exercises and simulations of the situations they're likely to face out in the field. This is not just the case for the team on the ground either. Those officers who will be controlling the mission from the situation room go through similar training. This, in essence, is what role playing is all about (albeit with less tanks and more demons).

Whether you play them on your computer, round a table or out in a field (referred to as Live Action Role Playing), this training will enable your mind to act and react instantly to tactical situations and will thereby increase your chance of survival.

There is only one thing to bear in mind when partaking in role-playing simulations and that is that your opponents are alive. Whether it is a games master or other players — each situation that you are placed in will have been created by another sentient being, whereas when you are out in a real-life apocalypse your opponents will be very much dead and incapable of intelligent thought and planning (very much like those beer-drinking footballers we were discussing earlier actually). They will have no plan, they will be erratic, disorganised, unrelenting and without any battle strategy. You'll need more than a wooden sword, a latex helmet and 300 power points to beat them in the end.

SAFE HOUSE

Your 'safe house' or 'sanctuary' or 'sanctum sanatorium' (if you're feeling particularly pretentious) can be just about anywhere as long as it is secure from the amassing hordes outside. But like most aspects of the housing market, there are certain attributes that make some buildings more attractive to potential survivors than others and therefore a better choice to build your base of operations. Here are some of the things to keep an eye out for when on the hunt for that perfect locale:

Altitude

You are always going to be safer from zombies if you are higher up due to the fact that zombies can't jump (this applies to all creeds of zombies and not just the white male ones). Neither can they negotiate ladders very successfully, concoct a scheme to raise themselves to your height, or fly.

Of course, when we refer to altitude we are not talking about a shed on a hill. More suitable would be any room, apartment or office above ground floor – the higher the better, in fact. Being up high also limits the points of entry for the undead as they can no longer gain access through windows. That leaves only the doors, and if you block off the stairways that lead to the floor you live on it will create more barriers for them to breach before finally reaching you.

Points of entry/escape

You require a safe house with as few points of entry as possible. If there are ten doors leading into the building then that is ten doors you have to barricade and guard. It is also preferable to have 'bottleneck' entry points: small or normal-sized doors that are situated at the end of a corridor. This will mean that should that point of entry be breached, only a few zombies at a time can get through – and should you kill them, in time their bodies will essentially block up the door so other zombies can't get through.

As well as the regular points of entry into the building, you should also have an irregular planned escape route that doesn't involve doors and windows. This can be an attic to rooftop escape; cellar to sewers or through air vents to a different part of the building. This alternative escape route is essential because although the undead are mindless creatures, as we discussed beforehand, they are 'aware' of their surroundings. They will know that doors and windows are the best point of entry to a building and will be amassing outside of them trying to get in.

Once the dead have discovered you are inside a building, it is pointless trying to escape through the normal routes.

Windows

The fewer windows the better. In fact, no windows would be a bonus. If the dead can't see you, then it will be less likely that they will discover you. If your safe house does have windows then you can always consider covering them up, but if you have chosen to set up shop in a ground-floor building then a few sheets of newspaper stuck to the glass will do nothing to stop the undead smashing their way in should you make too much noise and alert them to your whereabouts. Your best bet, if on the ground floor, is to brick the windows up or barricade them as effectively as you barricade your doors.

Furniture

You are not going to survive if your safe house does not have a reasonable amount of items with which to barricade doors and windows. Choosing an unfurnished building as a sanctuary will mean that you will have to locate and bring items to it in order to barricade the doors.

Rooms

It is a common misconception that an open-plan safe house is more effective than one with many different rooms. You need as many accessible rooms as possible to give yourself a better chance of survival. The reasoning behind this is twofold.

Firstly, if the main door to your abode is breached by the undead you can simply set up a barricade at the next doorway. If you were in an open plan room you would have nowhere to run (apart from your irregular escape route – but here is the second part of my reasoning).

Secondly, if a zombie sees you head into an air vent or through a hole in the floor it will follow you – thus making your irregular escape route pointless. In an open-plan room a zombie is liable to spot you making good your escape, whereas in a multi-room safe house you can have your escape route set up in another room and thus make your escape without being spotted.

As a point of caution, it is preferable to have the bulk of your supplies in the room furthest away from the main door where the hordes are liable to gain entrance purely so that they are always accessible to you.

Location

Although in cities and towns you are more likely to amass better supplies, it is preferable to have your safe house in an area that has a lower population. Small towns or villages are ideal, or even business parks that have been built on the outskirts of a town. Lower population means fewer zombies – and also less chance of you getting nuked (see **Nuked**).

SKY FLOWERS

Or, as people of sound mind prefer to call them, fireworks. Some believe that if you shoot fireworks into the air zombies will be distracted by the shiny, pretty lights and you will be able to pass by them unseen as they all stare up into the night sky. They may even go 'Oooooh' and 'Ahhhhh' at the same time – who knows?

Other techniques that may distract zombies are shooting flares in the sky, dressing someone in a fibre-optic suit and making them dance on top of a building, giving them tickets to the *Fantasia* water and light show at MGM studios or shouting 'Hey, look over there!' whilst pointing behind them.

Please feel free to try any or all of these techniques if you wish and let me know if they work by sending a copy of your death certificate to my publisher's address.

SLEEP

I'm not even going to bother going into this. Of course you need to sleep. If you need me to tell you that you need to sleep then there is seriously something wrong with you. The human body needs sleep to be able to operate properly, and I know it may be difficult to get forty winks with the thought of shambling corpses outside, but you will have to. Sleep, that is. Because I don't know if I mentioned but you need to sleep.

Hey! You also need to breathe. Maybe I should have put a segment on that in the dictionary. Make sure you breathe. Yes? Should I go back and put it in now or should I just not bother? Tell you what, I won't bother and we'll just forget about this whole silly sleep incident, shall we? Just make sure it doesn't happen again, OK?

SOUNDTRACK

Music can be an excellent motivator, but if there is an apocalypse raging outside, we wouldn't recommend playing any tunes at full volume to pump yourself up prior to battle for the obvious reasons (it will draw the undead to you). Neither would we endorse using an iPod, MP3 player or a Walkman cassette personal stereo as this will plug up your ears and leave you open to a surprise attack. Instead, we suggest that you invent a playlist of music in your head that you can 'play' as a soundtrack for your life as you go about your daily business of surviving the undead. This technique has two points in its favour:

Firstly, the aforementioned motivational aspect of music. Studies have proved that music played both before and during intense workouts has improved the performance of athletes by, on average, 23%*.

Secondly, whilst you are imagining music playing in your head you aren't really allowing your brain to think about all the horror, blood, guts, gore and undeadliness that is occurring around you – thus desensitising your own mind and allowing you to complete your tasks more effectively.

The music you decide to use in your own personal 'soundtrack' is completely up to you as you will be the most aware of your own personal musical preferences – but here are a few suggestions of styles of music and individual songs that you can utilise for specific situations.

Preparation for Battle

This is when you should be playing any music that can be described as 'high octane'. The average bpm (beats per minute) should be anywhere between 120–140. Rock music is better than dance music at this stage as the guitar solos and middle eights with their power chords, key changes, and tempo can instil a sense of anticipation and power.

During Battle

You need something with a bit more kick, unrelenting pumping, non-stop action. This is where dance music will come into play. Don't go for the watered-down chart fodder, though. You need a bouncing, happy hardcore baseline to get you through an unrelenting battle with the zombie masses. Alternatively, if you are doing battle with a large stick or broom handle as your weapon of choice then add 'Me Ole Bamboo' from *Chitty Chitty Bang Bang* to your soundtrack.

After the Battle

You've won, and a sense of relief and exhaustion washes over you. As you make your way back to safety, remember that this is only one battle you have won. There's a long way to go yet before the war is over, so don't go for anything too cheery and upbeat. Maybe, 'We've Made it Through the Rain' by Barry Manilow or 'We've Only Just Begun' by the Carpenters. Allow yourself to relax.

Fortifying Your Safe House or Any Other Task of Importance

There's nothing like a good Eighties montage sequence to get you through these sometimes dull but extremely important tasks. Get the theme from *Footloose* playing in your head and that job will be over before it's begun.

Saying Goodbye to a Dying Friend

You can go for the obvious choices at this stage like 'Candle in the Wind' by Elton John or 'My Heart Will Go On' by Celine Dion; or how about that old karaoke favourite 'I Will Always Love You' by Whitney Houston? But, let's be honest, they're all a bit cheesy and also slightly depressing. Maybe you should go with something a little more ironic whilst your best friend lies dying in your arms. How about 'I Used to Love Her' by Guns and Roses or 'We're All Gonna Die Someday' by Kasey Chambers? That'll lighten the mood slightly.

*I made this percentage up purely to add weight to my argument because I couldn't be bothered to actually look up the official results of the trials. I'm sure it should be somewhere around that figure though and please feel free, if anyone should find the real results, to immediately email me so that we can update our future editions with the correct information. The address is doilooklikeireallycare@nomail.co.uk.

SPEED

OK, gang! It's hot potato time. Now, I know for a fact that the real zombie enthusiast and survivalist will have skipped through the rest of the book to get to this entry first. They will probably be reading this in the shop to ensure that I know what I'm talking about prior to purchasing the book. That is how important this particular topic is in the world of zombie survivalism. If you didn't skip to this bit of the book first and are now feeling devalued as a reader then just put the book down and pick it up and skip straight to this bit and then we'll just pretend that's what you did when you first got the *Zombie Dictionary* home. No one will know any different. It will just be our little secret. You'll know next time though, won't you? Speed is the big debate in apocalypse town so here goes: let's talk about the speed of zombies.

Do zombies move fast or slowly? It is an interesting question and if I am to answer it correctly then we need to base this on scientific fact rather than what is 'artistically preferable' for the genre of zombies in the media.

The truth of the matter is that zombies would mostly be slow moving. The degradation of their muscles, bones and body overall would severely limit their movement and it would be highly likely that given time, and depending on the speed of that degradation, a zombie will actually become slower and slower, eventually coming to a halt and collapsing. That's not to say it wouldn't attempt to keep moving by dragging itself along the floor but even then, that would be a slow process.

This means that 'newer' zombies will have the edge on their more rotted counterparts and this is where I'm going to be a bit excitable and off the wall. Depending on the time it takes for a corpse to reanimate and the health of the person prior to death, it is likely that there will be a limited period of time when a zombie will be capable of moving at the maximum speed it did when it was a living person.

Allow me to explain before you set this book alight and then attempt to seek me out to do the same. If we are to follow a scientific approach to zombie survival, rather than completely relying on the mythology and films surrounding the myth, we need to look at what happens to a corpse in real life – or real death.

Once a person dies, lividity will begin from between twenty minutes to three hours from the time of death. This is where the blood, which is no longer being pumped through the body, will sink to the lowest point in the body and pool there. Rigor mortis will also set in at around three hours after death. Both these factors will aid in slowing the zombie down. With blood pooled in its legs and stiff limbs they will not be able to move very fast at all. But neither of these things occur until three hours after death. If a corpse were to reanimate prior to this three-hour deadline, there is the possibility that at the onset of their reanimation zombies will still retain their normal speed until rigor mortis, lividity and rotting begins.

Remember, though, that zombies will only retain the maximum speed that they had when alive, so a young, healthy zombie would be able to move much faster than an old, feeble zombie.

Speed is an important debate in the world of zombie survivalists and some of those more avid fans of the subject have become so convinced of their own belief that they are unwilling to entertain the possibility of another point of view.

That is not the way of the true survivor. Let me reiterate.

The apocalypse has not happened yet. There has never been an account of a corpse rising. We do not know with any certainty what will happen and what form mankind's nemesis will take. We must be prepared for anything – even if that goes against our very beliefs – and scientifically there is the possibility that some zombies may not be slow. Bear that fact in mind – or you could end up dead. Very quickly.

SPIDERMAN ZOMBIES

The undead cannot climb up walls or walk across ceilings on their hands and knees. Neither will they be vegetarians. Silly Jeffrey Reddick (although kudos for *Final Destination*).

STICK

The ultimate fighting weapon. Do not let anyone tell you otherwise!

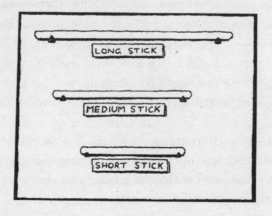

It can be found almost anywhere, comes in varying weights, sizes and colours to suit any survivor and can be adapted to be a multi-purpose bludgeoning and stabbing weapon merely by whittling the end to a point. If you don't have the means to do this you can snap it at an angle and the break should form a point (this then becomes more than just a stick, this then becomes the BPS – big pointy stick. You will be truly blessed to own one of these).

The stick is one of the safest weapons a survivor can own with minimal danger of causing damage to yourself whilst using it. Apart from a few splinters and unless you accidentally fall on the point or hit yourself in the face with it, you are highly unlikely to sustain any injuries from the use of a stick in battle. More people are killed worldwide each year by accidents with their own guns than accidents with their own sticks.

Depending on the length of the stick it can also be used to aid walking or to carry goods (you could sling it over your shoulder like Dick Whittington or across both shoulders like a coy but alluring milkmaid).

You can break windows with it, force open doors and cupboards. You can even cut notches on it to count how many days have gone by/zombies you've killed/yellow cars you've seen. You can use it as a measuring pole, or to check how deep water is, or to prod things to see if they're dead. You can knock things off tall shelves with a stick as well as use it as a back scratcher when you get an itch in a particularly hard place to reach. You can catch fish with it and play lawn darts. You can draw maps in the sand and also use it to pole-vault over walls and fences. There are many other uses for the humble stick, and if you can name me any other weapon that is as versatile then I shall eat my stick. (Eating sticks is not one of the many uses of a stick as our bodies cannot digest the cellulose. I was merely being pedantic as I know for a fact that you will find no other weapon that is as versatile as a stick. Not even a Swiss army knife. You just try using the very small screwdriver to kill a zombie – or the nail clippers.)

STUPIDITY

Don't, for god's sake, let stupidity be your downfall during the apocalypse. The zombies are supposed to be the stupid ones, not you. Here are the simple rules of thumb regarding the use of intelligence during a zombie apocalypse:

1) If you hear a noise then don't stand and shout a tentative 'Hello' and then proceed to go and investigate said noise whilst continuing to repeat the word 'hello'.

2) If a cat or other small animal leaps out making you jump then you can assume that anywhere between 10 seconds to a minute later a zombie will leap out and attack you.

3) Should you go out on a scavenging mission and on returning to your safe house it seems deserted, do not walk slowly into the safe house calling out for your teammates – especially if the place has been ransacked and the lights aren't working. Leave immediately.

4) If you then discover one of your teammates silhouetted in a doorway or in front of a bright light and they do not respond the first time you call their name, then shoot them in the head or run. They have been transformed! Don't get any closer and especially

don't take the time to say their name sadly and shake your head in sorrow.

5) On entering a dark and scary room alone, do not put your weapon and/or method of communication down on a table and then walk over to the other side of the room as far away as possible from it.

6) If you get into a car or any vehicle to escape from an attacking zombie and the car doesn't start immediately then get out and find another means of escape. Don't just sit there repeatedly turning the key and listening to the engine splutter.

7) When given the choice of either escaping into the relative safety of a house or trying to lose a zombie in a dark forbidding-looking forest, choose to hide in the house.

8) If somebody says to you 'You don't want to go in there...' then please, dear god, trust them. You really *don't* want to go in there.

9) When being chased, do not stumble around gasping and panting and squealing every time you trip over a tree branch. Just climb up a goddamn tree! Zombies can't climb! From that point you can come up with a more comprehensive plan that doesn't involve gasping, panting, squealing and rolling down leaf-covered embankments straight to the feet of your attacker.

10) If you hear any form of music that involves tense violin chords or a rumbling slow tempo playing when you enter a room, building, street – then you can guarantee that something bad is liable to happen. Also, if fog rolls into the street for no apparent

reason this also means that something bad is about to happen. Likewise, if your torch batteries suddenly fail, it's a sign that something bad is going to happen. If you spot any of these signs then back away from the location you are in and go someplace safer that has nicer music and no fog.

SYMPTOMS

Although there has been no recorded outbreak of the zombie virus yet we can make some simple assumptions as to what some of the symptoms may be that will indicate that a person is going to reanimate as a zombie. Bear in mind that the depiction of the zombie virus in films, books, television and other media is based purely on speculation and that there is equal possibility that none, all or only some of the symptoms that the characters portray may occur when a person has been infected by a zombie virus.

The zombie virus may take many different forms. It may take days, hours or minutes from the time a person has become infected to the time that a person reanimates, so the length, speed and duration of any symptoms that an infected person exhibits may vary and cannot be guaranteed either by scientific fact or conjecture.

Thus far, here is the list that we have managed to compile of the symptoms of a person infected by the zombie virus prior to reanimation:

1) Death.

2) Actually…that's it…

We can guarantee beyond a doubt that a person will, in fact, show acute signs of death prior to being reanimated as a zombie. Unfortunately, currently this is not a good symptomatic indicator to the fact that a person may reanimate purely due to the fact that most human beings (and in fact all living organisms) will suffer this symptom to some degree of seriousness at some point in their life. With this in mind, should you come across a person who is suffering from death then please do not automatically assume that they will reanimate as a zombie. Death is only one of the symptoms that is associated with the zombie virus. Unfortunately, we haven't been able to pinpoint the others yet. But as soon as we do, you'll be the first to know.

TEETH

The second-best alternative to saving yourself from being infected with the zombie virus (the first being the destruction of the brain, for those who haven't been paying attention) is to take out the blighter's teeth. If a zombie has no teeth then you can't get bitten.

The handy thing about teeth is that they are situated quite near to the brain, so if you do miss the brain you could possibly take out the teeth instead (or the nose – but that's not very handy as the zombie virus is not passed on through touching a zombie's nose). Either way, repeated blows to anywhere around the facial area should do something that will aid in neutralising the zombie threat so stick with the original plan of going for the head.

> **NOTE:** The virus will not be passed through the teeth. It will be passed from the *saliva* in the mouth. Removing the teeth will merely cause an open wound through which the virus may pass into your bloodstream. If a toothless zombie was to bring its mouth into contact with an open wound on your body you would still be infected.

THE BEGINNING

The reason that this is listed under T is because the beginning of the apocalypse will never just be known as a beginning. It will always be THE beginning. With the obligatory capital T.

When the apocalypse gets underway, it's important to understand that it won't be a slow-burning affair that will idly work its way across the world as government bodies and authorities fail in their task to keep their countries safe and secure. When it hits, it will hit hard and it will hit fast. You could go to bed one night with the world at peace and in relative harmony and wake up the next morning with buildings burning, bloodied bodies piled high, the streets in chaos, the wail of the injured, gunfire and sirens piercing the air, and nuns running naked through the streets.

Likewise, you could step from the calm and peaceful streets of your town into a restaurant to grab something to eat and by the time you had finished your steak and ale pie with curly fries and had left the building, the main road could be in uproar with overturned cars, the undead chewing on the living, blood-smeared shop windows, store alarms piercing the air and nuns running around naked.

Equally as likely is that you could leave your desk in your open-plan office to go for a quick wee. After you've finished relieving yourself you may return to your desk only to find severed limbs strewn across the carpet, furniture upended against doors, your workmates either dying, dead or reanimated, the sprinkler system and fire alarms going off and nuns running around naked.

What you need to learn from these examples is that when the apocalypse does begin you will have little or no time to gather your thoughts. You must be ready to react immediately to the situation and be capable of putting all the survival techniques you have learnt into immediate action. There will be no time to react to the horror you are witnessing. No time to take in the scenes of degradation. Of complete chaos. Of death and destruction. And certainly no time to take in the naked nuns.

THINGS YOU MAY NOT HAVE CONSIDERED

There are those of you out there who will be completely ready for a zombie apocalypse and are just reading this book to cross-check your own plans or to shake your head in nerdy disgust and disagree with me (remember the apocalypse hasn't happened yet, so where's your proof that I might be wrong? Ha ha!)

Then there will be those of you who are using this as the first step to discovering a life of survival after the undead rise.

In both cases, though, there may be things that you haven't considered – and even if you have considered them there will be people out there who haven't so let's just stop being so smug and self-righteous for the moment whilst I deal with the others.

Generally speaking, your main role in the apocalypse is going to be fighting, scavenging and surviving, but there will always be something in your well-thought-out plans that you hadn't considered. Of course, I couldn't possibly comment on what that might be because I am not privy to your personal survival preparations, but think for a moment what you might have missed out of your contingency plans.

I carried out that very same thought process the other day and do you know what I realised? Do you? That we would run out of cheese. Might not seem earth-shattering or of great importance but cheese is going to be scarce during the apocalypse and I like cheese. Nothing fancy, just your bog-standard mild Cheddar. But all the same, I like it and there's not going to be a lot of it around when the undead rise. So, by considering this eventuality now, I can ensure that I have prepared myself for that disappointment come the apocalypse, meaning I will be of a stronger disposition with or without cheese to calm my nerves.

Another thing that the majority of zombie survivalists don't consider is that they could be wrong. They have a theory on the undead, they have a plan to survive and they are going to argue the point and stick to the plan at all costs. Sorry to say this chaps and chapesses but you have to consider the fact that you may not have it right. The apocalypse hasn't happened yet so we have no proof whose thoughts and theories are correct – you are going to have to consider the fact that your whole survival plan may have to change at a moment's notice because you were wrong. Hey! Even I might be wrong – and if that's the case – why bother reading this book or paying any attention to what I say? Because at the end of the day – there's just as much chance that I'm right too. You know what I'm saying, eh? Now, go on, away with you. Go and bulk buy cheese.

THRILLER

Before I get started on this entry, this is by no means a personal dig at Michael Jackson and I would never speak ill of the dead, unless they were undead, and I don't think he's undead. Although he may well be 'not dead' and working with Elvis and Princess Diana in a chip shop somewhere, but that's a whole different kettle of conspiracy theories which isn't worth thinking about so we'll get back to the point.

Over the years many things have been said about the private life of the king of pop and these speculations should be left well enough alone by the serious survivalist as we cannot hope to overcome the apocalypse by pinning our hopes on scurrilous gossip and scandal-mongering. And a morbid fascination regarding eccentric celebrity's foibles is certainly unhealthy to say the least. That said, Mr Jackson will probably be accountable for a great many deaths during the apocalypse and that's not idle gossip. That's fact.

In 1983 he single-handedly managed to ridicule the terrifying phenomenon of zombies and turned it into a cult obsession. Yes, I'm talking about the music video of his chart-topper 'Thriller' which became an instant classic. The dead are shambling towards us, growing ever closer. They're coming for our flesh. They're coming, they're coming! They're dancing! Ah, look, the dead are dancing! Isn't that sweet? Let's all join in. In fact, I had absolutely no sense of rhythm before – but maybe if I become a zombie I'll be able to dance like them! Quick! Bite me!

If you put anybody in zombie make-up you can guarantee that within seconds they'll be doing the 'Thriller' dance, lifting their legs and arms up and down in jerky movements from left to right, grinning like buffoons and expecting everyone to applaud riotously as if we'd never seen it before. On film sets they do it, at zombie walks, Halloween parties, even funerals (not very often at funerals – but occasionally). It needs to stop now! The nation has become desensitised to zombies. They no longer fear the undead – and no matter how many new zombie films come out and no matter how horrific they are, the 'Thriller' dance always rears its head to ridicule the undead again and make them seem safe. It may seem trivial now, but come the apocalypse, as people watch and wait for the zombies to dance, they will realise all too late that zombies have no rhythm and do not dance. And then they'll get shredded and it'll be all the king of pop's fault. Michael Jackson is very bad. And not in the good sense as in the song 'Bad', but in a bad way that actually means bad... See what he's done! He's even buggered up the English language.

TIME

Time will become relative during the apocalypse. One day will blend into the next and, as there will be nothing to plan for and no dates that desperately need remembering, time will become unimportant. As the clocks slowly wind down and the electricity shuts off, the only indication you will have as to whether it is night or day is whether the sun is in the sky or it is dark outside. Minutes, hours, days, weeks, years: they will all merge into one. There will be no time anymore. It's a scary, scary thought. But at least it gives you an excuse for not buying a Mother's Day card.

TRAMPOLINE

A portable trampoline can be used by your good self to gain access to the first floor of buildings without having to go through the front door. Simply set up the trampoline under an accessible window and bounce up. Once you have finished you can jump back out of that window again, land on the trampoline and be on your way. Be aware, though, that should you run into a zombie in the building you have accessed and you push it out of the window to protect yourself, that it is liable to bounce back up again and again and again and again and again... You get the point.

TRANSFUSION

If the idea crossed your mind that on becoming infected you could possibly have a full blood transfusion in order to save yourself then bear in mind that once the virus has travelled through the blood and into the brain you are beyond help. During a transfusion the blood is pumped out of your body (quite possibly passing through the brain) whilst the new blood is pumped in, meaning that a transfusion will be a little bit of a waste of time. I also believe that I may have mentioned just once or twice before that: THERE IS NO CURE! Why do I have to keep repeating myself to you people?

TRAPS

OK, why would you even think about trapping a zombie? The idea is to kill them, not keep them. You're not thinking about that children's entertainment business again? Dressing them in silly hats and making them dance? How many times do I have to tell you? It won't work! What? You wanted to know about making traps to catch animals that you could use for food? OK. What kind of animals? Something between five and six foot with two legs and two arms... Do I look stupid? You cannot use zombies for children's entertainment! Or as fluffers for your amateur porn either.

TRIP WIRES

Would you be daft enough to fall over a piece of string that was tied across the bottom of a doorway? Of course you wouldn't. Putting trip wires across doors was the kind of thing that Dennis the Menace did. It was a childish prank that no self-respecting adult would ever fall for in a million years. It is tantamount to putting cling film over a toilet seat, or glueing all the tissues together in a tissue box, or putting a dead sparrow in your grandmother's hotpot that she was making for the family dinner. Silly, silly, childish games.

Unlike these silly, silly, childish games, though, trip wires can be effective against the undead because zombies really aren't as clever as us normal humans. A zombie will be focused on its prey so will pay little attention to what is tied across a door. If the trip wire is attached securely enough it will send a zombie toppling over and give you time to escape or bring your foot down on its head. If there are multiple zombies it will cause a pile-up of corpses, again allowing you to escape in the ensuing confusion. If you have the correct supplies you could even make the trip wire out of barbed wire or cheese wire. This way the zombie may lose his feet and give you even more chance of either defeating him or escaping. It is with this in mind that we recommend setting up trip wires throughout your safe house. As an added bonus don't tell anyone else you are doing it – watching your teammates fall over every time they walk into a room will cheer you up in the dark days of the apocalypse and will also give you advance warning of who you may wish to get rid of early on in your survival regime before they slip on a banana skin and get you all killed.

TROUSERS

Not wishing to be at all sexist, this segment can apply to any form of clothing worn on the bottom half of a human being. It includes, but is not limited to, skirts, kilts, shorts, leggings, jeans, pantaloons and nappies. It was just easier to list it under the heading **Trousers** as it saved me the trouble of listing all the other possible leg adornments which I actually did anyway. Please note, then, that when I refer to 'trousers' or 'pants' in the following paragraphs it will also include (but is not limited to) all the other items listed above.

'Being caught with one's pants/trousers down' is an old saying that means you have been caught unawares doing something – it is also an old song by AC/DC that can be utilised in your pre-battle soundtrack (see **Soundtrack**). Imagine, though, if you were literally caught with your trousers down (or indeed off) when the zombies attacked your safe house. Perhaps you were in bed? Perhaps you were on the toilet? Maybe you just decided to give your legs some air, or were partaking in a thigh-measuring contest with the rest of your team (Eton rules of thigh-measuring contests require you to remove any clothing from your legs as thicker materials can give a false positive reading)? Whatever the reason, you have no pants on – what would you do?

On hearing the undead breaking down the door, most people's initial reaction would be to grab a pair of pants and pull them on. But let's consider the facts here. *The zombies are at your door.* Do you really have time to start pulling on your best chinos? Is that really the best use of your time when corpses are invading your house?

Test the theory. Remove your pants now and place them at the other side of the room. Now, see how long it takes you to put them on. Now pick up your weapon and prepare to fight. How long did that take? Thirty-five minutes! What do you mean thirty-five minutes…? Oh… OK, well, how long would it have taken if you hadn't realised *Emmerdale* was on and you stopped to watch it? You don't know? You're not taking this very seriously, are you? I'll tell you how long. Our tests showed it could take someone up to two minutes to put on a pair of pants (longer if they were a tight-fitting pair of skinny jeans) and that is time that is wasting whilst the zombies get in.

There are many situations where pants are important and even a necessity: going to work, popping to the shops, giving a talk at your local primary school about traffic safety. But what real use is a pair of trousers when fighting zombies? Trousers don't imbue you with extra power; trousers won't scare the zombies away; they don't have special armour built into them (unless they are armoured pants – in which case my argument becomes somewhat moot).

The bottom line is that you don't need trousers to fight zombies. So next time you are caught with your trousers down, leave it that way. Just be glad you still have your underpants on (or, so as not to be sexist, knickers).

> **OR...**
>
> To avoid never being 'caught with your trousers down' you could simply never remove your trousers. However, bear in mind that it will make visits to the bathroom quite difficult. Actually, best just to discard that idea – unless you plan on putting a flap in the back of your slacks.

UMBRELLA

Insert in the zombie's mouth and open it up to create a cascade effect of blood, guts and bits of brain whilst also stopping any of the above splattering onto your newly scavenged Kate Moss collection party frock. Who said that zombie killing couldn't be fun and inventive at the same time?

Umbrellas can also be used to stop you getting wet and as a mode of transport to traverse large hordes of the undead if you happen to be practically perfect in every way.

UNBREAKABLE

Picture the scene. You are happily scavenging away in a deserted Aldi warehouse, stocking up on your supply of processed German sausage and sliced cheese with holes in it, when all of a sudden a zombie appears from behind a crate of half-price violins. (Excellent value, I bought one. Strictly to use as a bow and arrow set – see **Musical Instruments**.)

Anyway, the zombie has appeared and you make a grab for your axe that is attached to your handy workman's belt. As you pull it free, the belt snaps and falls to the floor. The zombie advances! You raise the axe in the air and the head flies off leaving you with naught but a piece of wood. The zombie moans and advances some more! You decide that you probably shouldn't fight the zombie with a stick and decide to run, but your shoelace snaps and trips you over. You try and get up, but due to the previous issue with your workman's belt your trousers have fallen down. The zombie is now almost on top of you! You back away into a corner and grab your radio to call for help from your friends outside, but the aerial has snapped off!

Then the building falls down on your head and the universe implodes!

Naturally, it is unlikely that a person would have that much bad luck at any given time, but in these days of mass consumerism, companies are making their goods more disposable and less durable, meaning that you could be left in a rather sticky situation at any time should a weapon or tool you are using suddenly break.

This is why, prior to the apocalypse, we recommend stocking up on *unbreakable* items. Not every company in the world has gone down the route of producing shoddy merchandise and there are the few out there who are continually keeping their standards high by flooding the market with supposed unbreakable goods. You'd imagine this was rather bad business sense because if they never break, you'll never need a replacement. Once everyone who wants one has got one they're never really going to sell anymore as generation to generation the unbreakable wonder they have manufactured is going to be passed through the ages.

A cursory glance through the interweb shows that you can get an unbreakable cafetière (that serves four), an unbreakable juicer, unbreakable golf tees, unbreakable tent pegs, unbreakable laptop bags, unbreakable thermal lunchboxes, unbreakable coin tubes (with screw tops), unbreakable combs, unbreakable mannequins, unbreakable clutch levers for Honda dirt bikes, unbreakable rosary beads, unbreakable multi-coloured kazoos (packs of 12) and unbreakable Christmas tree stars from Italy. The possibilities are endless and should you stock your safe house with all these unbreakable items then you will never have to worry again about being let down on the battlefield or at home.

UNDERGROUND

Most zombie survival manuals will tell you that it is unwise to head underground when the apocalypse has begun and that you should get as high up as possible to avoid being attacked by the undead. This is good advice. Advice that I have also given out on a regular basis, but there is one thing to bear in mind when you make your sanctuary at the top of a great big building that is surrounded by zombies. How are you going to get out to stock up on more supplies?

There is the possibility that you could use bed sheets or stapled together bits of old newspaper to construct a basic parachute or hand glider but these can be difficult to steer and could land you in the middle of a horde.

If you are an adept tightrope walker this is also an option, but how are you going to get the tightrope attached at the other end? And don't even think about walking across a telephone line – they can't even carry calls sometimes.

Finally there is the option to jump across to the adjoining building. A small gap may just be manageable but should you miss and plummet to the ground below, I'm sure that may hurt just a bit.

If you have managed to secure a safe location from the ground floor up though, your safest option is to create a subterranean tunnel system, one that attaches to sewer systems, tube lines, ancient tombs and other such undergroundy places.

It is a common misconception that you will run into multiple zombies if you venture underground. If a zombie is not reanimated in an underground area then there is no reason for it to head there. Once they have carried out their initial carnage, zombies are more liable to migrate across land in order to seek out bands of survivors to attack and are highly unlikely to accidentally end up in a storm drain en masse (see **Migration**).

That is not to say that you will not run into any of the dead if you use pre-existing underground tunnels. There is always the possibility that one or two of them may have ended up down there, so do still be vigilant.

The same rules also apply regarding panic zones (see **Panic Zones**) and any underground areas attached to hospitals or escape routes (e.g. subway stations, airport car parks) which may also be heavily infected.

This won't be a problem, though, if you dig your own tunnel system. All you need is a basic knowledge of the area you are in and a good idea of where you want your tunnel to end up. You will also need something to dig with (your hands will do if you can't find a spoon) and something to stop the roof of your tunnel caving in. If you do not dig the tunnel deep enough then zombies are liable to fall through the floor into your tunnel and gain access to your safe house – don't say I didn't warn you, as I'm not being held accountable should you end up making a botch-up of your great escape plan.

Once you have perfected one tunnel you could consider the possibility of creating an entire network of tunnels that connect safe houses and supply locations across the city. You could even build huge underground caverns where you can house millions and hold mass raves before heading off to fight your oppressors. And you could call the place Zion. And ruin a perfectly good trilogy in the process. Actually let's just stick to one tunnel for now. From your safe house to Kentucky Fried Chicken. The brave new world can wait.

UNIVERSE

You may consider the idea of blasting off into space when the zombies attack the earth; of entering the final frontier; putting together a motley crew of adventurers to travel across the universe to seek out new life and boldly go where no one has gone before, but you will run out of food and water and air and you will all die and then possibly reanimate and then there will be zombies in space. I hope you're happy.

URBAN AREAS

If you get the chance, then get out! Urban areas, although filled with abandoned shops full of supplies and empty buildings where you can locate your safe house, are the least attractive places to be when the zombies rise.

Urban areas have a high population of people in them at any

one time. Either, working/shopping during the day or working/partying at night. This means that should the undead begin to rise in that area then there will be a large number of zombies who may or may not migrate once the initial outbreak has subsided.

Due to this high-density population, you may also get nuked (see **Nuked**). What are you still reading this bit for? The explanation is under **Nuked**, like I just said.

Disease is the final reason to move on out. The number of dead – reanimated or not – and the associated rotten stench, will make living in urban areas almost unbearable, especially in the summer months when the tightly packed buildings and pollution residue will increase the heat and smell to levels of disgust that no person has ever endured before. All this rotting human flesh will attract insects that will spread the diseases and you will become ill and ultimately die and then rise again and start rotting and add your own aroma to that disgusting stench that will lie over the urban areas after the apocalypse has begun.

Your best bet is to set up shop in the suburbs and organise snatch and grab raids during the winter months when the smell would have subsided slightly due to the cold and rain. Ensure that you carry out reconnaissance first (maybe with your highly trained sheep – see **Animals, Training of**). It's important for you to be aware of where the undead have horded and which streets aren't blocked by debris and abandoned cars.

You will also need to get as many supplies as possible to last you through the oncoming summer. Because the cycle will repeat itself year on year and the smell will just get worse.

VANS & LORRIES

When you think of a safe house, you imagine it to be a highly secure location that is on the top floor of some building with heavy fortifications surrounding it. And you'd be right to think that – those are all ideal criteria for the perfect safe house. However, have you given any thought to having your safe house in the back of a van or lorry?

Naturally, there is the issue of fuel to be taken into consideration when thinking about having a fully moveable sanctuary but should you be able to overcome that difficulty by accessing an alternative fuel source – such as alcohol, biomass, wood, gas, steam, compressed air, cooking oils, peddle power, hydrogen or liquid nitrogen, to name a few (there are a lot of alternative fuels about) – then a moveable sanctuary is just as good an option as a fully secure stationary one, as long as it is fortified correctly.

Size does matter when considering a moveable home. You cannot just hook up a caravan to a hatchback and hope for the best. Should you be attacked by zombies, a reasonable number of them will be able to tip your caravan over with no problem at all.

If we're honest, enough zombies could topple any vehicle but we shall gloss over that fact as I like the idea of a moveable sanctuary – especially in the back of a juggernaut like in *Knight Rider*. And this brings us to the perfect vehicles to use for moveable safe houses: security vans or police vans. If you can get your hands on a police or army control centre van then even better (as they've got radios and televisions and chairs in too).

All these vehicles are heavy, which will make it more difficult for the undead to tip you over, and they also generally have armour-plating that will stop hundreds of grabbing hands and beating fists putting a dent in the side. This means that minimum customising will be necessary, apart from the fuel source. You may want to put a cattle grid on the front and you will also have to make the driver's cab accessible from the rear area, if it's not already, along with adding support and security to the windows of the cab to keep the driver safe.

The only issue with these vehicles is that you will have to ensure your team is kept to a minimum, as the only way you will be able to accept more members is if you create a convoy. But more vehicles would attract more attention and more zombies on your tail.

The alternative, should you wish to make more room, is to trade up your van for a big red AEC Regent 'RT' double-decker bus and then you could ride across country and across the Channel to Athens with Hank Marvin, Bruce Welch and Brian Bennett whilst being chased by a girl's mother and agent as well as zombies too. You've seen it in the movies, so let's see if it's true.

VENTRILOQUISM

The art of throwing one's voice. A very useful technique to have when you are being attacked and need to draw a zombie away from you. Please do ensure that you have practised this technique before using it in a real-life defensive situation. Mumbling 'gottle of geer' through clenched teeth will do nothing but make your final moments on this earth look slightly ridiculous.

Also note that you do not have to have a dummy to be a decent ventriloquist and walking around with your hand stuffed up a small wooden man's bottom will do nothing to instil confidence in you from your team.

VOX POP

'Well, to be honest, I think it's disgusting that our council allowed this to happen. Ten years ago you'd have never seen this kind of thing happening in Chorlton. The house prices have just plummeted since the zombies have taken over and no one cleans up their own dog poo either.'

FZZZZZZT

'It's immigrants, that's what it is! Immigrant workers! First they take our jobs, now they die and eat us! The world's gone mad!'

FZZZZZZT

'Yeaaaaaaah! Props to the Fleetwood massive!!! Yeeeeeahhhhh!'

FZZZZZZT

'My mum says that we should think of all the people who are suffering and she said I should sing... *Love lifts us up where we...*'

FZZZZZZZT

'My favourite cheese is cheddar. It's the simplest of cheeses, but simple is sometimes best. Don't even get me started on Wensleydale...'

FZZZZZZZT

'...and then when I heard what Vera had told my Barry I just couldn't believe my ears so I had to see it for myself. So I went outside and it was disgusting. Blood and arms all over the place. Tell them, Barry, tell them – he'll tell you. All I can say is we won't be going to that particular Chinese Restaurant again...'

FZZZZZZZT

'Cock! Tee hee, tee hee...I said *Cock!*'

FZZZZZZT

'I like long walks in the country and visiting new and interesting places and ultimately I'm looking for a woman who will share my passion for pre-war politics and grass... What? This isn't a dating service... You want my opinion on the zombies? No. I don't fancy one of those...unless they give out on a first date...'

FZZZZZZZT

And ultimately this is why the general public should not be allowed to speak or pass opinion once the apocalypse begins.

WASTE DISPOSAL

This is one of those things that generally goes under the radar when considering how to survive a zombie apocalypse. During the training and planning stages people focus solely on how they are going to keep on living and kill all the zombies simultaneously.

But within this never ending circle of survival there are also the menial tasks that need to be addressed and this is a task that could ultimately cause some problems.

In our everyday life, it has become somewhat routine to empty the bins on the assigned day and just wait for the bin men to come and pick up any waste that we have amassed over the week. During an apocalypse there will be no bin men.

So where will all the rubbish go? You can't leave it lying around the safe house, as this will cause hygiene problems and disease amongst your team.

It is also not too clever an idea to just dump it out of a window to land in the streets below as the same rules of hygiene apply. Plus, over time, the waste product will start to smell, making your safe house unliveable.

An ever-increasing pile of rubbish outside your safe house can also cause two other possible problems: Firstly, other survivors may spot the 'fresh' rubbish and be alerted to your safe house; and they may not be the kind of survivors you want discovering your location.

Secondly, over time the pile of rubbish will get bigger and bigger and bigger meaning that eventually the undead may be able to scale the rubbish heap and access your safe house through the window you've been throwing it out of.

You also don't really have the option of sending one of your team out to dump the rubbish at a safe distance away, as you don't want to risk the life of one of your team purely with the job of putting the bins out. You can't burn the rubbish either as this may attract the attention of the undead. So? What do you do?

Recycle! That's the only thing you can possibly do. Yup. What our rather pointless councils have been using as a smokescreen to confuse us into ignoring the larger and more important issues over the years could be the only way to stop your safe house turning into a cesspool of disgust.

Some Useful Tips on Recycling:

Firstly, any paper or card can be used to insulate your walls and windows and can even be used as an extra layer of covers for when you are sleeping at night (if it's good enough for drug-addicted homeless people then it's good enough for you).

Tin cans and metal containers can be turned into weapons (have you ever cut your finger on a soup can lid? They are lethal!)

With regards to food waste, there shouldn't be any of that, not if you are truly intent on surviving. You should be munching through every last item on your plate. Even the sprouts.

The only other item of waste to consider after that is human waste, and it may be prudent to consider that the flush facility may become inoperable during a zombie apocalypse meaning that you won't be able to dispose of your waste as easily as you first anticipated. Not wishing to get into poo too deeply (ahem), there are two possible solutions to this problem.

1) You could go down the route of 'humanure' whereby you recycle your own waste product to be used at a

later date to help grow new foodstuffs in your cellar. Do bear in mind, though, that it can take up to two years for human waste to break down into purely organic matter which can be used for composting. During that time you will have buckets of poo standing around covered in sawdust or straw (which apparently reduces the odour according to the *Humanure Handbook* (available to download online in multiple languages).

2) You could utilise your other waste products to construct a rudimentary slingshot (e.g. an empty baked beans tin within a large crisp bag). You can then catapult your waste product from the roof of your safe house to a reasonable distance away. As long as you are not spotted, any zombie that may be alerted by the noise the tin of poo makes when it lands will not have the mental capacity to work out where it came from, leaving your safe house uncompromised. And in a best-case scenario you may hit one of the undead blighters on the head.

Frankly, I would be more inclined to go with the second option regarding the disposal of human waste, but if you really do feel like doing your bit to save the planet by all means surround yourself with containers of human waste for months on end. The one consolation is that should other survivors discover where you are hidden, they certainly won't want to invade your sanctuary – unless it's Kim and Aggie. Then you'll be in trouble.

WATER

'Let us head for an island! An island will be safe from a zombie attack!'

'But we're on an island. Britain is an island and it's not safe'

'No! I mean a smaller island, like that island in the middle of that lake over there! The one that the park keeper always shouts at us for taking our peddle boats too near!'

'Oh yes! What a good idea! Let me just go and get my speedos on so we can swim across – the park keeper will only shout if we get a peddle boat too near.'

OK, let's see if we can spot what's wrong with this conversation. Yes, OK, we'll ignore the bit about the speedos. Speedos are most definitely wrong whether we're in a zombie apocalypse or not. The issue here is the statement that an island will be safe. Will it? Will it indeed?

Zombies cannot swim. They are incapable of doing the backstroke, butterfly or even the doggie paddle and would be unable to keep themselves afloat, let alone stay in their own lane.

However, that does not mean that zombies aren't able to come into contact with water. Remember, a zombie is dead so it doesn't need to breathe. What's to stop a zombie just walking through the water and onto your safe little island? That's *through* the water and not *on* the water – zombies are not Jesus and as I think we've already explained, neither is Jesus a zombie.

Due to their state of death, zombies' bodies are capable of withstanding a lot more than the average human being. As long as their brain is not adversely affected, they will be able to walk through anything to get to you, be it poison gas, a floor full of nails, a field of nettles or a vast amount of water.

So, armed with the knowledge that an expanse of water is not a safe barrier from the undead bear these facts in mind:

1) Zombies may become trapped under water due to rubbish or plant life that they get tangled in – making them an unseen enemy. If you are swimming across the water they may grab you from below, or if you are in a boat they may attempt to capsize it.

2) They go where the current takes them. If a zombie wanders into an area of high current, as long as its head isn't smashed against the rocks it could be washed up on the shore anywhere ready to carry on marauding – maybe even the island that you believed was so safe.

3) Saltwater will aid in the destruction of a zombie. The heavier the salt levels the quicker the corpse will degrade – and as water will get to the brain via various orifices in the body, the brain will also be destroyed too. Fresh water will actually slow the decomposition down. Corpses that are left in water will actually rot slower than bodies left on land, so although the water will disfigure and bloat the zombie, it will ultimately extend its life longer than if it was on land.

4) Just like on land with insects, there are scavenger fish that will eat away at a corpse thus doing your dirty work and destroying the undead for you. Depending on how old the corpse of the zombie is and how far the flesh has rotted, sharks and piranhas could also be tempted to eat a zombie if it ventured into the sea.

5) If anyone were ever stupid enough to start a zombie zoo, the safest way to exhibit them would be in tanks of water, like in the Sea-Life Centre. The zombie will be unable to climb out of the tank due to the glass sides and the water would also slow down his movement even more than his natural shambling gait.

6) You could also consider the option to use water as a weapon, or at least as a means of defence, should you have an ample enough supply of it. Police and the authorities have been known to use hoses for crowd control in riot situations and there is no reason why a strong current of water blasted at the undead should not hold them back too. As they are

rotting flesh, the force of the water may be strong enough to clean the meat from their bones making it more difficult for them to walk. You could even be lucky enough to wash out their skulls and clean away the brain.

7) The final point to make regarding water is that, as far as survival is concerned, you are really going to need a supply of it. For a period of time, you may be lucky if the main water supply stays active. Do not count on this fact, though. On hearing of an apocalypse you should start stockpiling water. Fill up all available containers. Even fill up the bath. Then ensure that you ration it for as long as you remain in that particular area. And the first person you find in the bath surrounded with bubbles and playing submarine with the shampoo bottle, stick a spoon in their ear. Really, really hard.

WEAPONS

Throughout this dictionary you have been taught one simple fact about weaponry and that is that ANYTHING can be used as a weapon. With that in mind I am not going to list all items that could be used, as that would just involve a very long list and you may as well just buy a real dictionary and look through all the nouns because every single one of them can be used as a weapon in some form or another.

Instead, I'm going to go through the subgroups of weapons to give you a better idea of how each of these nouns can be operated for maximum devastation and effectiveness.

Long range

Long-range weapons are those that cause damage without you having to be near your victim. These fall into two simple categories: targeted and non-targeted.

Long-range weapons such as guns, crossbows and missile launchers tend to have some form of crosshair or targeting system on them meaning that they are liable to be more effective in hitting your intended zombie.

The disadvantage of these weapons is that they are generally two-part weapons – in other words, they require ammunition to operate. The non-targeted long-range weapon is one that can be propelled towards a zombie but does not have a targeting system, so in order to be effective it requires skill or luck. Such weapons include spears, rocks, clocks, pens, chairs, books – in fact, anything that you are strong enough to pick up and throw. These items can also be used in conjunction with a catapult, either the kind Minnie the Minx used in the *Beano* or the one the French used to throw the cow in *Monty Python and the Holy Grail* (thus showing the effectiveness of anything being used as a weapon).

Medium range

These are non-propulsion weapons that will cause damage to your victim up to a range of between 3 and 6 feet, including gems such as scythes, spears, big pointy sticks, whips, lengths of chain, fishing rods, coat stands and standard lamps.

They are generally useless once your attacker gets too close, purely due to the length and the manoeuvrability. However, with quick thinking these can be broken down or grasped further down the shaft in order to cope with closer attacks.

Melee

Close combat weapons. Although allowing a member of the undead to get too close to you is inadvisable due to the risk of infection it is always handy to keep a melee weapon on you. A melee weapon will generally fit in your pocket or on your belt and is effective at short-range strikes (e.g. katana, kitchen knife, hammer, rock, candle-stick or lead piping).

Stabbing

The stabbing weapon has a point and is able to puncture. The point does not have to be metal and it could be glass, wood or even plastic whittled to a point. The focus of choosing a good stabbing weapon is whether the point will be able to penetrate a skull. It is all well and good choosing an item with a weak blade and planning to go through the eye socket or ear, but what if you miss? You may only get one chance at this.

Bludgeoning

The easiest weapon to find, as all you do is hold it in your hand and strike down on the zombie's head. As with the stabbing weapons, the focus with this weapon is whether the striking force would be strong enough to crush a zombie's head in one blow. A stuffed womble can be used as a bludgeoning weapon, but it may take one or two strikes in order to break through the skull and destroy the brain.

Live

Animals can be used as weapons, but remember when sending a dog to attack a zombie that the zombie will probably eat the dog. More effective live weapons are pools of piranhas and those beetles that they use in *CSI* and *Bones* to strip corpses of dead flesh. If a zombie fell into a pit of those it would be stripped bare in a day and will no longer be a threat (just don't fall in yourself). You can also class throwing your little sister at a zombie as both a long-range and live weapon.

Damage

Damage weapons will not be capable of doing the job of destroying a zombie's brain, but may slow the zombie down in order to facilitate your own escape. Explosives fall into this category (see **Explosives**) along with any weapon that may decapitate or remove limbs from the zombie but not kill it. A huge bag of stuffed wombles dropped on the zombie thus burying him would also be classed as a damage weapon as it will slow him down leaving you time to escape.

Slow-acting

Weapons that will kill a zombie, but not immediately. You will need to be at a safe distance or have a quick escape route planned in order to use these weapons. Corrosive acid burning through a skull takes time but will ultimately do the job.

Although fire is a hazardous option for you to use as a weapon (see **Fire**) it will eventually burn a zombie away to nothing so is therefore very useful.

Pointless weapons

Although it is possible to use absolutely anything as a weapon, sometimes it does take time to come up with a reasonable plan to turn the items in your possession into zombie killing mechanisms. Bearing that in mind, there's no need for you to carry a box of confetti and a bottle of Ribena with you just because I told you that anything can be used as a weapon. It is much better to arm yourself sensibly in the first instance and only become inventive when the need really arises. Then you can make your confetti-Ribena killing machine – can't think how, although I bet the A-Team could. Or MacGyver.

WEATHER

You put on a coat and take an umbrella when it rains. You wear shades and shorts when it's hot. You put on a scarf and mittens when it's cold. Currently, the only way most of us are affected by the weather is by planning our daily wardrobe around what mother nature throws at us. Trust me, though, when the apocalypse takes hold the weather will help and hinder you in equal measure and it will become much more than a topic for small talk with the cashier when you're buying your egg and cress sandwich on your lunch break. Consider the following:

Rain

Most of us see rain as a bit annoying. It gets us wet and makes leaving the house an unpleasant experience. However, in a zombie apocalypse, our perception of the weather is likely to be flipped on its head.

Rain will have many plus points. First, it is water and it is falling from the sky. Water will be in short supply. The mains supply may have become compromised, you'll have scavenged every bottle of Evian from the local stores and drinking your own urine is will have become repetitive. So, when it starts to rain, simply place a few buckets on your roof and you will have all the supplies you need.

Rain will also have a cleansing effect on the area around you. Bloodstained streets will be washed clean and chunks of rotting flesh will flow down the gutter, helping to remove things that may cause disease and smell.

From an aesthetic point of view, rain will also clean up any zombies that are caught outside in it. Removing dirt and congealed blood making them easier on the eye and less terrifying to look at.

Rain will also help things grow should you be trying to cultivate your own foodstuff in a safe area of your sanctuary.

Do be aware that rain isn't always a good thing, though. As basic drainage systems degrade due to lack of upkeep, flooding will become more likely. This may compromise any areas that you inhabit on ground floors or below (see **Underground**) but as long as you keep high and your building is strong enough to withstand a flood, you should be safe.

Heat
As I said, our perception will be flipped on its head and intense sun and heat will no longer be something we look forward to.

Prepare to dread those hot summer days – ice-cream and building sandcastles will be a thing of the past. Long periods of heat will cause drought and will mean that you will find water supplies harder to come by. Heat will also cause lethargy and exhaustion in your team members, especially if there is a low supply of water. High temperatures will aid in the rotting process, and although this will speed up the demise of our undead friends, it will also increase the smell of rotting meat and increase the amount of disease-spreading insects which will be buzzing around.

The only good thing about the sun is that you will get a lovely tan, which will stop you being mistaken for a member of the undead by other survivors.

Cold

In extreme cold temperatures, zombies will freeze. This does not mean that they will 'die'. It means they will freeze solid and then reanimate again once they have thawed. The unfortunate thing about this is that you will also freeze in extremely low temperatures and you are unlikely to carry on as normal once you have thawed out – because the extreme cold will have killed you. In cold weather it is best to stay within your safe house and attempt to keep warm until the temperature heats up as cold weather can slow down a person's response time and, like heat, induce lethargy.

Snow will also be a problem. Zombies will become buried in snow banks meaning that you have to be extra careful when making what would normally be a simple walk down the road as you don't know what could be concealed beneath the blanket of snow. If snow can be collected, though, it can be melted down to increase your supply of water.

Fog

Do you really think it's a good idea to go wandering out into thick, pea-soup fog when there's an apocalypse on? Do you not watch horror movies? Or any movies for that matter? Fog isn't good. It holds all kinds of scaries. Including, but not limited to, zombies. That you can't see. Because of the fog!

Extreme weather

With a big red X as warranted by the cable TV show title. Typhoons, hurricanes, tornadoes, force ten gales; all these extreme weather conditions are generally associated with certain places on the planet. Surely it would be sensible then, should a zombie apocalypse occur, to move out of an area that is likely to have a typhoon season or is regularly battered by hurricanes. I know that it might be home. But what are you trying to prove? You just have to survive. You don't REALLY have to survive. No one's going to be impressed if you survived the zombie apocalypse AND a tornado. It's not a competition. Hey! Once you've got through the tornado why not move to San Francisco and see if you can survive an earthquake too! And there's an active volcano in Skamania County. Then you could go to space and see if you could get through a supernova. In fact, once you do, why don't you just stay there, eh?

WILDCRAFTING

What was once the simple art of foraging in the wild for edible plants has now become a minefield of ethical and ecological legislation and laws that could land you in more trouble than eating the wrong kind of mushroom. You would imagine that all of these laws about preventing the extinction of certain species, retargeting what you sow and ensuring sustainability will become null and void whence the dead do rise and begin eating us, but you can guarantee – irrespective of the calamity to hit earth – there will always be some bleeding heart tree-hugger knocking about spouting on about the error of our ways, the raping of the planet and how we must leave this earth the way we would want our children to find it. I'm going to go out on a limb here and make a suggestion should you come across one of these jolly sorts on your travels, hit them with a shovel.

As it stands, I completely believe that the human race is doing a damn fine job of buggering up the planet what with its continual urbanisation, pollution, global warming and sucking the land dry of all its natural resources whilst giving little or no regard to any other living creature in the process.

In fact, I can state with pretty much 100% certainty that mankind will in no small way be to blame for the rising of the dead due to one or all of the reasons listed above. I also think that these people who I previously referred to as 'bleeding heart tree-huggers' have a very valid point to make (which would be made more effectively by them if they shaved occasionally, washed once or twice and didn't wear hessian all the time) and god bless them for trying to get us all to come to our senses about the mess we're making of this planet we call home. But, once the apocalypse begins I'm afraid that it's every man for himself and sod the humble dandelion.

The tree-huggers' aim is to prevent species becoming extinct. So, by eating a dandelion, I am actually protecting the human race from extinction. You'd think that would please them, that they'd thank me for the effort I'm making to save myself and thus mankind? But no, you can guarantee that they will harp on about sustainability (they love the word sustainability – almost as much as they love the word ecostructure, and they love that word a lot) that is why they need to be hit with a shovel and then fed with that very same shovel to the zombies. The undead also need sustaining so that they don't become extinct too. It's the circle of life my tree-huggy friends. For one species to survive, another species must become dinner and I can assure you although I make my donations regularly to Greenpeace and WWF (World Wildlife Fund, not World Wrestling Federation – John Cena does not need my money), come the apocalypse, if the need arises I would roast a giant panda over an open fire and serve him up with side order Arakan forest turtle if it ensured I would survive.

Note: In the event a giant panda is unavailable, nettles, wild rose and Japanese knotweed are also edible and a lot less endangered.

WINDOWS

'Oh! Look outside, look, there are zombies!'

'Shouldn't we really board that up?'

'No. Look. There are some zombies.'

'Yeah, I know. That's why I think we should board it up.'

'But we need to look outside. At the zombies.'

'Well, can't I board it up and just leave a gap to look through?'

'We wouldn't be able to see many zombies through a little gap, would we?'

'I've got some wood or some sheet metal…'

'We need to be able to see how many zombies there are outside.'

'There are lots of zombies outside. We know there are zombies outside. Why do we need to see them?'

'Because if we can't see them how do we know they're there?'

'Because it's a zombie apocalypse?'

'Oh! Look! They're coming to say hello! We wouldn't have known they were going to come in through the window if the window wasn't there would we? Hello? Hello? Where've you gone?'

XYLOPHONE

OK, I know that I've been through musical instruments in this dictionary previously, but give me a break. There's not really that many things that begin with the letter X so I had to use my initiative and Xylophone seemed to be my best option, otherwise we'd have been talking about the X chromosome which could have opened up a can of worms with those folks who believe that all gender should be abolished (talking about scientific proof of gender difference can sometimes put the willies up these folks).

Or maybe I could have tried Xerox but frankly the only use for a photocopying machine during the apocalypse is to either drop it on a zombie's head from a great height out of a window (and as we've already discussed, using a heavy item for zombie killing is never a sure thing); or you could while away a few hours of boredom by photocopying your own face and/or genitalia.

Besides, I'm not even sure I can use the word Xerox as it's a copyrighted trade name so I would have had to put any of that advice under 'Photocopier' which I wouldn't need to because I had ample entries for the letter P.

The Xylem is plant tissue that conducts water and minerals from the root to all other parts of the plant and, as interesting a fact as that might be, it's really not important information to have when considering your own survival during a zombie apocalypse. Then, of course, there's the X-ray – a machine that operates by using radiation. Just trust me, keep away from it. You'll do more damage to yourself than you could ever think of doing to a zombie with the radiation from an X-ray machine. Which frankly, only leaves me with Xylophone to work with and is vastly more useful than any of the other X words because it can be used as a bludgeoning weapon and will naturally make pretty music as you batter the zombie's head.

YMCA

First, just let me tell you that there's no need to feel down, there's quite an easy and accessible way to pick yourself off the ground and especially if you happen to be relatively new in the town (that's none specifically, *any* town) there's really no need to be unhappy because there is actually a place you could go that will deal with all the aforementioned woes that could have befallen you, especially but not exclusively if you are short on your dough. You can stay there and there are also apparently many ways in which to have a good time (again, which particular good time you will be privy to isn't specified, but we are assured that whatever time it is that you have, it will be classed as 'good'). Where is the wondrous place? Well, it's a place called the YMCA or the Young Man's Christian Association.

Heavily endorsed by the leather-clad biker, Indian, policeman and cowboy of the Village People fame (which surely pleased the Christian aspect of the YMCA no end), this institution helps young people improve their mind, body and spirit both mentally and physically (much like what I am attempting to achieve with my survival training, except that they don't talk quite as much about the undead as I do). They also help young people by dealing with issues such as homelessness, crime, education and families.

As important as their work is in building community spirit and helping young people succeed in the world today, the only thing that people identify with when you mention the YMCA, is the dance. You work hard putting together a charitable organization for 160 years and all anyone can ever remember is that bloody dance!

The dance can be used for both a simple exercise routine or as a short choreographed movement in battle that when repeated can kill multiple zombies.

THE YMCA DANCE

Y: Holding your arms aloft will set yourself up as an open target to a zombie and it will move forward to attack.

M: Bringing your hands down in an inward sweeping movement, grab the zombie's hair or ears, ensuring that its mouth is kept at a safe distance from your face.

C: Whilst still holding the ears/hair twist your arms into the conventional 'C' position. This will twist the zombies head from its body. Release the right ear, so that the head is raised at the top point of the 'C' once it is detached from the body.

A: Forcibly bring your hands together in the A movement. This will effectively crush the zombie's skull (and therefore brain) between your palms. Repeat as necessary.

For those who can't be bothered to train in any form of official martial art, this technique can be applied to most other movement-based 'party dances' for either attack or defence technique. E.g. *Agadoo, Around the Old Camp Fire*; *Court of King Caractacus*, *Time Warp* and the entirety of Steps' playlist.

YOGA

Staying supple during a zombie apocalypse is imperative. You never know when you will have to crawl down a U-bend, shimmy through a crack in the wall and worm your way under an overturned milk float to escape the undead hordes, and yoga is one of the best ways to ensure that your body remains the temple it's supposed to be.

Of course, there is no gain without pain, and likewise there is no pain without gain (however, there is rain in Spain which falls mainly on the plain) and if you want to be capable of putting your own foot behind your head whilst your hand rotates your spine, then you are going to have to spend time practising.

Although throughout the majority of this book we have advocated a regime of self-training, when it comes to yoga, it would be vastly more sensible to receive one-on-one professional training, so that you don't end up stuck with your head inserted in your back passage with no way of removing it, as you may need to escape down your back passage should a zombie attack begin... What? No, that's not what I meant – some people just have minds like gutters.

YODA

Bad zombies are. Them to kill brain the destroy them to win must you. Master am I of all knowledge Jedi. Though, speak properly I not, though even I am most clever and trust in I do you. Also sound I like Fozzy Bear. Still trust in me do you?

YO-YO

I hit you in the head! I hit you in the head again! Ha Ha! Hit you in the head again! And again! Now I'm walking the dog. And I hit you in the head again! Cat's cradle. And there's the head again!

YWCA

Young Women's Christian Association.

Nobody wrote a song about them. This is obviously quite a sore issue as they never mention it in public. Ever.

ZOMBIE WALKS

For those of you who aren't initiated into the world of the zombie fan life. A zombie walk is where a large group of people gather together and walk the streets of a city on a predestined route dressed as zombies. Although you may assume that these events would carry the same perils as Halloween, in many ways you would be wrong.

First off, the majority of people who take part in a zombie walk are zombie enthusiasts which means they know all about zombies and how to kill them and how to spot them and what to do should the apocalypse begin. So, they have no need to worry for their own safety either from zombies or from the authorities shooting at them believing they are the undead. And as soon as news of the apocalypse reaches their ears, they will go into hiding just like this book advises.

Secondly, zombie walks only entail a few thousand people whereas on Halloween the whole city will be dressed up. This means that the advent of the apocalypse will be easy to spot and those affected for real will also be easy targets. A zombie walk takes a predetermined route so anyone straying from this will be prime targets for brain destruction.

Finally, there is no way that anyone would mistake a zombie walk for a real zombie outbreak as 90% of the zombies in a zombie walk will have mobile phones, cameras, video cameras or other such recording devices to hand, ready to capture their jolly day out and upload to YouTube and Facebook as they go along. And as we all know, zombies don't have Facebook profiles and if they did their status would say 'Luv my m8s. U know who u r. Anyone up for a rampage:):)'

ZOO

Throughout this dictionary I have made various references to different species of animals and how they may be useful to you or not during a zombie apocalypse. Well, here we shall talk about where these cuddly little creatures reside: a zoo.

As a refuge during the apocalypse, a zoo has various pros and cons. There are a lot of animals there that could be trained to carry out your bidding and keep you safe. And there are a lot of animals there who will make a noise and draw the zombies to your location looking for fresh meat.

You can hide in one of the many terrained areas where each animal lives in its 'natural' manmade habitat. Monkey houses will be ideal places to hide as they have access to trees and high places (although the monkeys do tend to throw poo at you which can be quite disconcerting), and the caging or glass around these areas is usually quite high so that the monkeys can't get out (and thus the dead can't get in).

Apart from that particular enclosure, though, these days each animal is usually housed in a sunken area so that the public can look down upon them (and thus feel superior) or surrounded by water, thus making it quite easy for the dead to get to you either by dropping in or wading across. The majority of food in the zoo will also be geared towards feeding the animals and the only supplies you will be able to get your hands on are those that are sold in the over-priced cafeteria or ice-cream carts dotted around the place. (Of course, you could always have roast lion, but you'd have to catch him first and do you really want the bother? Maybe start with something easy like a penguin).

To be honest, zoos aren't very good places to hide at all, what with the lack of food and the chance you might be mauled and eaten – by wild animals as well as zombies.

There are also really tacky-looking baseball hats and T-shirts sold in the gift shops, along with the pencil toppers where you stick the writing implement up the badger's bum so it sits there whilst you write (and there aren't even any badgers in this zoo!). I frankly wouldn't even bother. Just nip in, grab a giraffe (see **Giraffe**) and be on your way.

Animals also live in safari parks. There is no way I would recommend you entering a safari park during a zombie apocalypse. The animals roam free and you would be much more liable to be eaten or mauled. You would also get the windscreen wipers pulled off your car, and baboons may defecate on your bonnet. All that and dealing with zombies too – it just isn't worth suffering the stress for.

DR DALE'S FINAL WORDS OF WISDOM

As I reach the 70,000-word quota that I am contractually obligated to write, I realise that today we have merely scratched the surface of the information that you will need to know when planning on surviving the coming apocalypse.

There are so many things that have been left unsaid. How could you utilise a bag of multicoloured rubber bands to aid in your survival? Can you use a tea urn full of pears to treat psittacosis? If a zombie fell down in the woods and no one was there to hear it, would it make a casserole? What role would a battologist play in your team? What role would a battologist play in your team? And would it be possible to move the entire human race to Mars?

Some of these things we will never know. Some of these things we will, and some of these things we really don't want to know the answer to. The important thing is not to dwell on what you haven't learnt but think about what you have and adapt that knowledge to expand your survival skills to suit any situation that may occur during an apocalypse. Without the capability to use your own common sense and come up with new and interesting ways to get through the dark days of the undead, I can assure you that you won't survive. You will get bitten and you will reanimate and then rise again and then get killed again by a much better survivor than you who was able to adapt, use their common sense and came up with new and interesting ways to survive. And I didn't spend three days on a beach in Malibu courtesy of my publishers writing this dictionary just for you to fail.

The twenty basic points listed overleaf are all you really need to remember if you plan on surviving a zombie apocalypse, which begs the question: why did you bother buying this book in the first place? Why not just nip into your local bookshop and steal this last page? It's a good question and I shall answer it for you. You bought this book because you have a quest for knowledge. A yearning to learn all there is to know about surviving the days of pain that await the human race. You bought this book because you know that the apocalypse is coming and that I am your only hope of survival.

Stay safe. Stay alive. Stay unreanimated.

Dr Dale
Seslick

You could also have purchased this book for the £10 voucher on the next page that can be redeemed at any outlet of Big John's Weapon Mart, but it's highly likely that someone will have just nipped into their local bookshop and stolen the last page. Bastards. They'll get theirs when the zombies rise.

DR DALE'S 20-POINT SURVIVAL PLAN

1) Zombies are dead.

2) Go for the brain.

3) Hide immediately on hearing of the apocalypse.

4) Get high… Actually I'll rephrase that. Get to a high place.

5) Don't get bitten.

6) If you do get bitten, kill yourself by destroying your own brain.

7) Be wary of other survivors.

8) There is no cure.

9) Anything can be used as a weapon (either defensive or offensive).

10) Choose a weapon that best suits your fighting style.

11) Zombies don't have supernatural abilities.

12) There is no cure.

13) It doesn't matter how the apocalypse began. It did. Deal with it.

14) Zombies can survive under water.

15) Steer clear of panic zones before, during and after an apocalypse.

16) There is no cure.

17) Many a muckle makes a muck.

18) Fail to plan. Plan to fail.

19) Zombies have no memory of their human life.

20) The cure can be found at Birkin Labs on the outskirts of Raccoon City. Ha! Just testing you… No, wait! Come back! That was just a test. There is no cure! Have you learnt nothing? Come baaaack! Oh Jeez, you're all going to die!

ACKNOWLEDGEMENTS

Amongst the many people who should be thanked are those folks who spent their time writing interesting stuff on the world wide web on the vast amounts of topics I needed to research in order to write this book – your knowledge meant I didn't have to leave the house once.

The lovely Lara at Allison & Busby who said yes to six pages of a website and now knows more about zombie survival than she ever wanted to.

David Ash and Jess Napthine who really had no idea what they were getting themselves into when they agreed to this.

The entire High Council at After Dark Entertainments most of whom keep me sane, but not necessarily grounded.

Jack Haysom – zombie slayer of the future.

My Mum, Dad and sister for immeasurable support and love.

And Lee Cooper – my own reason for wanting to survive.